THE ROAD TO XENU:
LIFE INSIDE SCIENTOLOGY

THE ROAD TO XENU:
LIFE INSIDE SCIENTOLOGY
Margery Wakefield

Copyright 2009 Margery Wakefield

ISBN: 978-0-557-09040-2

Have nothing to do with the fruitless deeds of darkness, but rather expose them.
> Ephesians 5:11

DEDICATION

This book is dedicated to all victims of the destructive cult of Scientology.

Excerpt from a Secret "Upper Level" of Scientology

"The head of the Galactic Confederation (76 planets around larger stars visible from here) (founded 95,000,000 years ago, very space opera) solved overpopulation (250 billion or so per planet—178 billion on average) by mass implanting.

"He caused people to be brought to Teegeeack (Earth) and put an H-bomb on the principal volcanoes (incident 2) and then the Pacific ones were taken in boxes to Hawaii and the Atlantic-area ones to Las Palmas and there 'packaged.'

"His name was Xenu. He used renegades. Various misleading data by means of circuits, etc., was placed in the implants.

"When through with his crime, Loyal Officers (to the people) captured him after six years of battle and put him in an electronic mountain trap where he still is. 'They' are gone. The place (Confed.) has since been a desert.

"The length and brutality of it all was such that this Confederation never recovered. The implant is calculated to kill (by pneumonia, etc.) anyone who attempts to solve it. This liability has been dispensed with by my tech development.

"One can free wheel through the implant and die unless it is approached as precisely outlined. The 'free wheel' (auto running on and on) lasts too long, denies sleep, etc., and one dies....

"In December, '67 I knew somebody had to take the plunge. I did and emerged very knocked out but alive. Probably the only one ever to do so in 75,000,000 years. I have all the data now but only that given here is needful....

"Good luck."

L. Ron Hubbard

Contents

CHAPTER ONE: Implant Stations in the Sky   1

CHAPTER TWO: Your Needle Is Floating!   11

CHAPTER THREE: For the Next Endless Trillions of Years   21

CHAPTER FOUR: Flunk for Laughing! Start!   31

CHAPTER FIVE: Do Fish Swim? Do Birds Fly?   45

CHAPTER SIX: On a Clear Night You Can See Forever   59

CHAPTER SEVEN: The Date of the Incident Is 520 BC   81

CHAPTER EIGHT: Star Trek for Real   107

CHAPTER NINE: Death on the Titanic   125

CHAPTER TEN: Find Out Who You Really Are   145

CHAPTER ELEVEN: Welcome to the RPF   167

CHAPTER TWELVE: Have You Ever Enslaved a Population?   185

CHAPTER THIRTEEN: We Are All Many   203

CHAPTER FOURTEEN: Back in the Wog World   221

EPILOGUE   229

CHAPTER ONE

Implant Stations in the Sky

It was a sunny, crisp day in late October as I slowly walked home to my little apartment on East Ann Street. The sky was a bright endless blue, and little gusts of breeze stirred the leaves on the sidewalk into small whirlwinds. Fall was my favorite season. I liked the nippy bite in the air that made me want to walk faster and brought the blood to my skin and hinted of impending frostier winter air.

As I entered the apartment, I looked around in satisfaction. I had been in this apartment only two weeks. The apartment was decorated on my meager student budget, but I didn't do badly, I thought, as I looked around. With two small cans of paint, I transformed a few old boards into a bookshelf, using some old bricks I found in the backyard. An Indian-print bedspread from the flea market covered the old, worn sofa. Another Indian-print fabric served as a tablecloth for the small table against the wall.

Anything Indian was "in" those days with the most "hip" students, the ones I worked with at the coffeehouse—like my friend Bob, who painstakingly taught me to do horoscopes. I spent my whole paycheck the previous month buying all the books and tables I needed to cast my charts, just like Tom, a philosophy major who introduced me to books by Edgar Cayce on reincarnation and past lives.

My friend Julie had a brash, cynical personality that contrasted sharply with my own shyness. She seemed to know everything about the world. Her parents were wealthy, and Julie always had the best of everything—the best clothes, the most expensive summer camps, even a car. She was schooled in Europe. Being accepted by Julie meant I was "in."

I knew Julie, because I had been assigned as her accompanist at the beginning of the semester. We were both in music school. She played the cello, and I accompanied her on the piano. We busily prepared for the recital earlier that day in which she played the *Lalo Cello Concerto.*

Everything went fine. Afterward, as she packed up her cello, she asked me to meet her for dinner at the Chinese restaurant on State Street.

"Sure," I agreed, honored by the attention of someone as popular as Julie.

Then she mysteriously added, "I have something important to tell you."

"Like what?" I asked.

Her teacher interrupted to talk to her about the performance.

"Later," Julie said with a small wave, dismissing me.

Relaxing on my sofa, I looked at my watch. I had plenty of time to reach the restaurant. I quickly changed into a wool skirt with a turtleneck sweater and an Indian top to wear over it. I wore my apple-seed necklace that I wore everywhere.

When I reached the restaurant, Julie was waiting. We found a small table against the wall.

After we ordered, I teased, "So what's the big secret?"

"Well, I want to tell you about something really important. This is the biggest thing that's ever happened to me. I have just made the most incredible discovery."

"What is it?"

"You remember the week I went to California to visit my brother about a month ago? When I didn't get back in time for Monday classes?"

"Yeah," I replied. "You sure have been acting different since you got back. You're never around the dorm anymore. Everyone's been asking what happened to you."

"You won't believe this when I tell you about it. It's too unbelievable."

"Well, tell me." I felt impatient.

"Margery, you have to find out about Scientology," she said intensely. "It's the most important discovery of the century."

"You're kidding." I looked at her incredulously. "That's the weird lecture we went to, where they had that little machine they hooked you up to. They asked if anyone wanted to try it. We laughed all the way home."

I remembered the night several weeks earlier when a group of us went to a free campus lecture on Scientology. The lecture was something about the mind, then the lecturer gave us a demonstration of a "meter" that was supposed to be able to read one's mind.

I didn't remember much of what was said at the lecture, but I remembered how we all laughed, as we walked home, mimicking the lecturer with his little brown box.

"Margery, listen," Julie insisted. "This is serious. It's too important to joke about."

"But you went to the lecture. It was silly. Being able to see into your mind with that little machine?"

"I know," she said softly. "I thought it was silly, too, but I went back the next day, because they said they had a free personality test, and I thought it would be interesting to take it. They took me to a house they all live in, and I saw a movie about Scientology. It explained how this is a brand-new science of the mind and how they could handle problems no one else could before. I really think you should find out about this," she said seriously.

"Like what kind of problems?" I asked uneasily.

"Look, this is a brand-new science. They have a whole new theory about the mind. It's a thousand years more advanced than psychiatry. They understand the mind like no one has before. They can get rid of all sorts of things—headaches, asthma, colds, anything, even cancer. It's 100% guaranteed. If it doesn't work, you get your money back."

"I wonder if it could help me with my anxiety attacks?" I muttered. I didn't know how much Julie knew about my problems.

"Sure. This is a science of the mind. If you really understand how the mind works, you can cure anything that's psychosomatic, right? The only reason psychiatry can't cure you is because they don't know how the mind works. If they did, they could cure you, but they don't. Scientology does."

I was quiet. No one at the dorm and none of my friends at the restaurant knew the extent of my problems. The previous year, my boyfriend died in a freak car accident. Too shocked to cry, I couldn't believe he was gone.

Shortly after the accident, I began having anxiety attacks in the middle of the night. I awoke covered in sweat and terrified. I couldn't remember dreaming anything before I awoke, but I always woke in a panic, sometimes frozen and unable to move. It occurred at least once a week. I feared I was going insane. Between attacks, I felt normal, although there was a general sense of uneasiness about something I couldn't identify.

I woke up screaming in the dorm one night, and Julie was one of the girls who appeared at my door, wanting to know what happened. Embarrassed, I told them it was a bad dream.

The second time it happened, the dorm mother insisted I see the school counselor. I had to see the lady once a week, and I found her a little strange. She sat there without speaking. I didn't like visiting her, but I didn't want the embarrassment of more screaming episodes, either.

That year, other things began to happen. Sometimes, I would be walking to class or to the music school to practice when I suddenly felt vaguely terrified, as if something horrible was about to happen. The feeling usually lasted a few hours, then vanished.

I felt uneasy. Something wasn't right. I was afraid of something, and I didn't know what it was.

"Do you really think Scientology can help me?" I studied Julie cautiously.

"If it's a problem in your mind, Scientology can take care of it. Anyway, what have you got to lose? There's no risk. If it doesn't work, you can go back to seeing your counselor. Yes, I think it can really help you."

"How do you do it? I mean, if I just wanted to try a little of it."

"First I'd have to take you to the center to get permission to audit you."

"To what?"

"To audit you. That's their word for what they do. It's like counseling, but it's called auditing. It's audit, because it has to do with listening."

"Oh. OK, I guess. How does it work?"

"Once I get permission to audit you, we'll go to your apartment, and I'll audit you. When I was in California, I took a course. Now I'm an auditor," she said importantly. "I learned more in that course than I have in two years of college."

"Do I have to be hooked up to that machine?"

"Oh, yeah. That's an E-meter."

"What's that?"

"It's short for electropsychometer. You hold onto the cans attached to it, and your thoughts register on the meter's dial. I'll show you exactly how it works tomorrow. You'll see. It really works."

We finished eating dinner, paid the check, and Julie walked me home. She came in, and we sat in the living room until 3:00 in the morning talking about Scientology.

She told me Scientology had been founded by an engineer named L. Ron Hubbard, who had unraveled the secrets of the mind. He was a wonderful person who just wanted to help mankind.

She said the central part of the organization of Scientology was called the Sea Org, short for Sea Organization. That was a group of mostly young people who lived on a fleet of ships in the Mediterranean with Hubbard, helping him reach Scientology centers around the world. The Sea Org's motto was, "We come back."

That, Julie explained, was because Hubbard and the Sea Org had come to earth thousands of years earlier to "salvage the planet," though at that time they failed to complete their mission. They returned to finish what they started to help save the planet from disaster.

Julie explained that, through auditing, everyone on earth could be "cleared" of their "reactive" minds, the destructive part of the mind that was responsible for all the suffering on earth—sickness, insanity, war, and people's negative experiences.

If, as Julie said, people could get rid of their reactive minds, there would never be sickness anymore. No one would be depressed, and everyone would get along. There would be no more war and fighting. Scientology made that impossible dream possible for the first time.

"If you really want to help other people," she said, looking at me carefully, "then you need to find out more about Scientology. As an auditor, you'll really be able to help people with their problems. You'll see miracles happen right before your eyes. I know. I've seen them."

"What kind of miracles?" I asked.

"Things like fevers going away, colds vanishing, people throwing away their glasses. I've heard stories in California that some people with withered limbs had them regenerate after an auditing session.

"There's nothing on this planet as advanced as Scientology. It's the beginning of something really incredible."

She told me about people she met in Los Angeles and how powerful they were. Some of them, she said, even had supernatural abilities. The ones who were "Clear" could travel outside their bodies at will and could read other people's thoughts or move objects by mind power. There were levels above Clear, called the "OT levels," where even more incredible things were possible.

"OT levels?" I asked. "What are they?"

"The OT levels are the ones above Clear." She explained the initials stood for "operating thetan," where the word *thetan* was the Scientology equivalent of the soul.

"There are eight levels above Clear," she said. "On those, you learn the secrets of this universe. You learn the history of the universe millions of years ago. You'll also learn about your own past, your hundreds of lives before this one. You'll learn to remember all of them."

Talking about past lives didn't bother me, because I'd been reading Edgar Cayce's books and was familiar with reincarnation. I could accept the idea of past lives, because many of my friends believed in them. Many of the people who worked at the coffeehouse were into Cayce and past lives, and it made sense to me. Maybe, that was why I had so much talent at the piano, I suggested to Julie. Maybe I played piano in a past life.

She nodded. "That's why playing piano is so easy for you. What you're really doing is remembering it from another life."

"Maybe, I knew Beethoven." I laughed.

"Who knows? Maybe you *were* Beethoven."

Julie said we all had hundreds of past lives, going all the way back to the old space civilizations of the past—history that wasn't recorded on the planet but was accessible through auditing.

"I'll tell you a secret," she said. "This is something I'm not supposed to tell you at this level. Earth is really a prison planet. Everyone here was sent here from another planet a long time in the past. All of us were either criminals, rebels, or revolutionaries from somewhere else. That's why this planet is so screwed up."

"But if all that happened to us, why can't we remember?"

"Because of the implants. When people were sentenced here, it was like being sent into eternal oblivion. It was the worst sentence you could get because of the implants. A long time ago, the implant stations were set up to keep us captive here, so we could never leave.

"These implant stations are white buildings out in space. When you finish a life here, you leave your body, but you're subconsciously programmed to return to the implant station. There, the memory of your recent life is erased with machines that emit high-powered electronic beams. Then you're programmed to return to earth for another life.

"You'll always return to the implant stations life after life. We've been doing this for millions of years."

"So what's different now?"

"Now there's Scientology. Hubbard's the first person in millions of years to figure it out. For the first time, in Scientology you can get rid of the return commands, so you don't ever have to return to the implant stations. Then you're free to go wherever you choose."

"Where would you go?" I felt dizzy with all that strange information.

"To another planet or galaxy. There are hundreds and thousands of worlds out there. There's no limit to what you can do. There's so much to see. It's exciting. Once you learn to 'exteriorize,' you can go wherever you want."

"What's exteriorize?"

"That's when you can leave your body whenever you want and travel anywhere in the universe. You just think of someplace, and you're instantly there. You can see and hear. You can do everything you do in your body, only better."

I was getting tired, so Julie stood and walked toward the door.

"I'll see you tomorrow at one o'clock," she promised, "for your first auditing session. See you then."

"Tomorrow," I agreed. "Thanks for the dinner."

It was hard to settle down and sleep that night. I had bizarre dreams about spaceships and strange sceneries, about white buildings in space with electron guns waiting to pin me to the wall.

That was my introduction to Scientology. Why did I believe such bizarre stories? Why was I so gullible? Why did no small voice inside me warn about possible danger?

There is no simple answer to this question. Part of the reason had to do with my chaotic and dysfunctional home. I grew up in a family where there was chronic discord. Sometimes it seemed as if my parents were too busy battling each other to notice me. I grew up feeling abandoned and alone. I learned to take care of myself, then later to help take care of my two brothers and baby sister, but there was never a solid foundation to my world.

Part of the answer had to do with the fact that I didn't have a strong religious background. I occasionally went to Sunday school, but that was usually a dull experience that I discontinued as soon as I was "on my own."

Part of the reason was that I was an adolescent, and, like most adolescents, I felt like I knew everything there was to know about life, while actually knowing very little. I was naïve. I expected adults to be wise and know the answers. I expected I could trust them. When Julie told me this man discovered some new science, I didn't question what she said. I'd been conditioned for seventeen years by my family and the educational system not to question adults. If they said they knew the answers, then they did.

Part of the reason was that I was vulnerable at this time. I was suffering from a form of mental illness that had been terrifying for me. The symptoms were strange and frightening. The possibility of finding an answer to this and an end to the suffering was the real reason that caused me to "bite." Once Julie promised me Scientology could give me relief, I was hooked.

Part of the reason I was so gullible was I was never warned. The word *cult* wasn't in my vocabulary. No one ever told me to beware of strange people with strange stories, free meals, or impossible promises. I walked into the trap full of trust and hope, never suspecting the noose was slowly being drawn tightly around my mind, trapping me unknowingly and unquestioningly in one of the most dangerous cults ever to exist.

CHAPTER TWO

Your Needle Is Floating!

The next day, I woke up wondering whether the previous night's events had been real or just part of a bizarre, elaborate dream. The answer came early that afternoon when Julie arrived with her E-meter in hand.

The meter was a rectangular box a little bigger than a cigar box, with two hinges on the side securing a removable top. We pulled my small table into the center of the room, and Julie set up the E-meter.

She removed the top of the box, using the side hinges to attach it to the back of the meter, where it became a prop to keep the meter at an upright slant facing her. The meter's face had a large dial under a plastic case with a thin needle resting at the left edge of the dial. During the session, Julie told me I'd sit opposite her at the table, where I wouldn't be able to see the meter's face. Only the auditor was allowed to see the needle *reads* that would indicate which part of a person's mind to explore, Julie explained.

First, she wanted to demonstrate the meter. As I stood beside her, she took two small juice cans from her purse and connected them to the leads attached to the meter and told me to hold the cans. Then she turned on the power. As she turned another knob, I saw the needle float lazily to the middle of the dial, move to the far side, and return to the left side.

"Your needle is floating," Julie informed me.

"What does that mean?" I watched the needle's lazy movements.

"When the needle is floating back and forth like this with no interrupted movements in either direction, it means nothing in your reactive mind is currently being restimulated. I'll show you. Watch the dial."

Suddenly, she pinched my arm.

"Ouch!" I wasn't expecting that, but the needle suddenly veered all the way to the right of the dial, even though I hadn't moved.

"Remember the pinch," she commanded.

As I mentally focused on the pain in my arm, the needle made a small movement toward the right side of the dial.

"See? The needle reacts to your thought," Julie explained. "The reason we use it in auditing is because we can see below your conscious awareness. When I ask you questions, the meter will give me your reaction at a subconscious level—things you may not even be aware of."

"So this machine can help you read my mind?" I laughed. "Amazing!"

I remembered how ridiculous the idea of an E-meter seemed at the lecture several weeks earlier and how we laughed about it on the way home. For some reason, now it didn't seem so silly. The way Julie explained it, it made sense.

"Are you ready to get started?" Julie asked, motioning me to the chair across from her. She took several sheets of blank white paper and a few pencils from a small portfolio she carried and set them on the table to the right of the E-meter.

"Sure. What do I do?" I felt that adventure lay ahead, and I was eager to start.

"Just hold the cans in your hands in your lap. Don't move them if you can help it. I'll ask some questions about yourself, and we'll see what happens." She gazed at me intently, glancing every few moments at the meter dial. "Tell me more about your anxiety attacks."

"Well, they started a year ago, right after Bill died. I was walking along the street one day when I began feeling terrified. It started in my stomach. It was as if something terrible was going to happen. I was too scared to move and just stood there. Finally, it went away, but it's been happening more and more. I seem to be afraid of something, but I don't know what it is."

"OK. That's fine." Julie wrote rapidly on the paper, as she spoke. "You had a read on the phrase 'a feeling of terror,' so that's what we're going to run."

"Run?" That was another familiar word used in an unfamiliar way.

"That means we're going to use a Dianetics technique to take this feeling of terror back to its root. Once we get to the earliest time you had this feeling, and you can reexperience that incident, the feeling should go away and never bother you again."

"How do you know if it's the earliest incident?"

"I can tell by the E-meter. The needle moves in a certain way when you've reached the earliest incident. Let's get started." She adjusted the knobs on the meter, then looked at me. "Locate an incident containing a feeling of terror."

"All right." I thought hard for a moment. "Yesterday, just before the recital, I started to experience fear. I had the feeling that something awful was going to happen."

"OK. What was the date of the incident?"

"Yesterday."

"All right. What was the duration of the incident?"

I thought back. "It lasted only about fifteen minutes."

"OK. Close your eyes. Go to the beginning of the incident and scan through it to the end, then tell me what happened."

I closed my eyes and followed her instructions. I saw the events of the previous day very clearly in my mind. "All right. I'm there." I described the event to her.

"Is the incident erasing or growing more solid?"

"It seems to be more solid." My eyes remained closed.

"All right. Is there an earlier incident containing a feeling of terror?"

"Yes. I had the feeling last week during a class." I began to visualize the classroom.

"OK. Move to the beginning of that incident." She asked me the same questions about the date and duration of the incident. At her command, I clearly visualized the classroom, and the familiar feeling of terror started spreading from my stomach to the other parts of my body.

"Is it getting more solid?" Julie asked softly.

"I think so. I'm starting to feel really scared."

"OK. Think back and see if you can find the earliest time you had this feeling of terror."

"I don't see anything."

"Just relax and see if anything comes to mind. It doesn't have to make sense. Just anything at all. Look for the earliest time you felt terror."

Suddenly, I saw the picture of a tiny foot and a hand in my mind.

"I see a foot. It doesn't make any sense. I just see this little foot and a hand, and I feel scared. I don't know what's happening." I looked anxiously into the darkness behind my closed eyelids, wanting to see more.

"All right. Go to the beginning of the incident and tell me when you're there."

"I'm there," I said uncertainly.

"Scan through to the end of the incident and tell me what happened."

"I see this little foot, and I see a hand, and it's pulling the foot. It's holding the baby upside down and spanking it. It's a baby that's just been born, and I feel scared, really scared. I feel like I don't know what's happening."

Julie looked at me expectantly without speaking.

"That's me, isn't it? That was me in the picture. I was being born, and I was scared." I opened my eyes and looked at Julie, wanting some kind of confirmation, but she just kept looking at me as if expecting something else. I closed my eyes again.

Then I noticed the terror subsiding, and I slipped into a state of deep relaxation. The picture faded into the darkness, getting smaller and smaller. Suddenly, I opened my eyes and looked straight at Julie and began laughing. It was as if I'd just heard the world's funniest joke. The laughter came from deep inside me, and I couldn't stop it.

Julie stared at me with a fixed expression, unsmiling, apparently not sharing any of my mysterious mirth.

After I sobered up, Julie stared at me and said solemnly, "I'd like to indicate that your needle is floating. This is the end of the session. You can put down the cans."

"That's it? That's all there is to it? You mean my anxiety attacks are cured?"

"You'll just have to wait and see. There might be other feelings involved." Julie turned off the meter, folded the sheets of paper, and started packing everything away. "I want to take you to the center. Come on. You have to see the Examiner."

We drove to an older house near the university. I still felt a lingering feeling of elation from the mysterious session.

As we walked into the house, I was directed to a small room off to the right with a sign over the door that read, *Examiner*. The middle of the room had a table with an E-meter already set up. A boy of high-school age sat at the table, and he motioned me to take the chair across from him.

"Pick up the cans," he commanded, looking at the meter and adjusting the knobs. He looked across at me and said solemnly, "Thank you. I'd like to indicate that your needle is floating. You can put down the cans." He smiled at my obvious confusion. "You have to see the Examiner after every session."

"Why?"

"Because if the needle isn't floating, or if the tone arm is reading too high," he pointed to one of the large knobs on the meter, "then you might have to go directly into a Review session, to correct whatever went wrong in your session. That's all. You're fine. Your needle was floating all over the dial."

He looked at me with satisfaction, then he stood, and I went to rejoin Julie in the hall. The boy handed Julie a piece of paper and disappeared into another room.

"Come on," Julie said. "I want you to meet everyone."

We walked into the living room where several people were sitting as if they were waiting for something. It reminded me of the reception area in a doctor's office.

Julie introduced me to an older woman who sat at a desk piled high with papers. "This is Rita." The woman smiled at me. "She's the director of the center." She looked toward several people sitting on sofas in the center of the room, who all seemed about my age or a little older.

"Margery just had her first session," Julie announced triumphantly.

"Wow, that's great. Congratulations."

Several of the people came over and hugged me or shook my hand.

"I can tell just by looking at you that it was a success." The older woman beamed at me, and she got up and took my hand. "Come on. I'll show you around the center. We have to get you signed up for the Communication Course."

"Communication Course?"

My question was lost, and she introduced me around. There were more hugs. Feeling like an honored guest, I responded to the friendly smiles and warm congratulations. I'd never seen so many apparently happy people. They could have been on drugs, but their eyes were clear and direct, and they had a relaxed alertness that belied any drug involvement.

Julie told me that we had to get a C/S before she could audit me further, explaining that someone called the Case Supervisor had to look over the notes she took during our session and give Julie instructions for our next session. The written page of instructions was called a C/S.

She explained that the other people in the living room are either auditors or their "preclears" who were also waiting for a C/S before they could resume auditing.

"I have some work I need to do," Julie said. "Why don't you stop back around seven tonight, and we'll see what's next? I'll meet you by the front door."

"OK. Thanks." As I walked toward the front door, I saw a small poster hanging in the hall with a picture of Earth drawn in crayons. Under it was a phrase in black that read, *What would you be doing if there were only seven days left until the end of the world?*

Strange, I thought, quickly dismissing it from my mind.

As I walked home, it seemed that everything was brighter. I felt unusually alert, noticing the bright, metallic colors of cars parked along the street and the unusual vividness of leaves on trees. I smoked marijuana a few times at parties, and this seemed curiously similar to the heightened perceptions I had when I was high on grass. Everything was more vivid.

At home, I went in the bathroom and looked in the mirror. Something caught my attention, and I felt a rush of euphoria as I looked at my reflection in the mirror. A thought formed somewhere deep in my mind, rising to the surface like a bubble.

That's not me. I felt simultaneously confused and elated. My mind raced ahead, as I groped for order to my thoughts. *That's not me.* Again, I looked into the mirror and my own eyes.

That's my body, but it's not me. I'm different. They're right. I'm not my body. I'm something else. I'm different from my body.

I felt as if the walls around me exploded and I looked around, but everything was the same. What was that explosion?

I decided to return to the Scientology house to talk to someone. Something was happening to me.

As I walked, the colors around me were unusually bright, and the euphoria remained. At any moment, I felt as if I might explode into a million pieces.

I walked up the steps into the house and found Rita talking to someone in the living room. Seeing me, she quickly came over.

"What is it?" She put her hand on my arm.

"I'm not sure. I just had a very strange experience." I told her about the colors and brightness on the way home, then my thoughts as I looked into the mirror and the strange explosion that followed.

"OK. You need to see the Examiner again and tell him exactly what you told me. It's OK." She smiled reassuringly. "Don't worry. This has happened to other people. You're just going a little faster than usual. That's all." She didn't seem alarmed.

A moment later, I again sat across the table from the young boy. Feeling somewhat embarrassed, I repeated what I told Rita.

He took notes as I talked. After staring at the E-meter for a long time, he looked at me with an expressionless face and said, "Your needle's floating. You can wait in the living room."

I sat in a chair on the far side of the room. Other people in the room were absorbed in reading or quiet, private conversations. I sat wondering what I was waiting for.

Half an hour later, the young boy appeared in the doorway with a manila folder in his hand. He shouted, "That's it! Margery has just attained the state of keyed-out Clear!"

People smiled at me and applauded. "Speech! Speech!" The clapping became rhythmical.

"Well," I stammered, turning red from the attention. "I feel really good. I'm not sure what's happened to me, but I feel great."

The applause continued.

Finally, Rita spoke from the doorway. "OK, Everyone. That's it. You can return to your reading."

The applause stopped as quickly as it began, and people returned to their previous activities. Julie came in with Rita, laughing as they approached.

I looked at them in confusion. "What in the world is keyed-out Clear?" I asked.

"It means," Julie replied, "that you've temporarily achieved the state of Clear. Sometimes, the reactive mind moves aside temporarily, and you actually feel like you would if you were Clear. I can't believe it happened to you after just one session!"

"Margery," Rita said, seeing my continued confusion, "the only way to really become Clear is to do all the grades in Scientology that lead up to Clear."

She led me to a large chart on the wall printed in red. Large red letters at the top read, *The Bridge to Total Freedom.* Rows of little boxes filled the chart. Each level on the chart represented a level in Scientology.

"You're here," Rita said, pointing to the lowest level. "Clear is here." She pointed halfway up the chart. "You must do all these levels in between to become a real Clear. However, because you've achieved the state of keyed-out Clear, I'm afraid that you can only be audited from now on by someone who's Clear or above." She motioned toward the upper half of the chart.

"What about Julie?" I looked at my friend, who stood silently beside me.

"She's not Clear, so she can't audit you here anymore. We don't have anyone here who's Clear yet other than myself. I'm Clear, but I'm not tech-trained, so I can't audit you, either."

"What should I do?" I felt even more confused.

"I'm afraid," she added with a broad smile, "you'll have to go to Los Angeles to continue your training. You've exceeded our ability to help you."

"I can't go to Los Angeles! I'm in school here!" I looked at them helplessly.

"Margery," Julie said slowly, "you have to decide. You don't know much about Scientology yet. It goes way beyond anything you can imagine. Look at the top levels." She pointed to a level just above Clear.

"These are the OT levels. When you get to these, you'll achieve states of mind that people before our time have only dreamed of. If you go to LA, you can train to become an auditor. This is the beginning of a great adventure for you, and there are no limits. There's no problem that auditing can't handle.

"Besides, didn't you tell me you wanted to help people? There isn't anything you can do that'll make as much of a difference as becoming an auditor. This is the most powerful stuff in the world—or the universe. Think about it."

I felt dizzy. Los Angeles? I considered my life in Ann Arbor. Somehow, things weren't the same. Working at the coffeehouse and attending classes seemed pretty dull compared to the events of the past two days.

It *was* an adventure. What did I have to lose? If it didn't work out, I could always return.

"OK," I announced. "I'm going to LA."

"All right!" Julie gave me a big hug. "This kid's gonna go Clear!"

"OK," Rita said. "We have to make some phone calls. Let's get busy." She looked at me proudly. "You have a wonderful adventure ahead. I promise you, you'll never be the same again."

CHAPTER THREE

For the Next Endless Trillions of Years

I stared out the window as the plane dipped into the greenish-yellow smog bank blanketing the city below. Five minutes earlier, the pilot announced our descent into Los Angeles.

I thought about the adventure waiting for me in the city that slowly materialized below, as we cleared the smoggy haze. I also remembered Julie's last words as we parted at the Ann Arbor airport. "Remember," she said with a smile, "the true test of a thetan is the ability to make things go right."

The past three days were a blur of activity. I had to withdraw formally from school, leaving behind a slate of incomplete classes. The record read, *Withdrew for personal reasons.*

I called my mother and asked her to come help me pack. "I'm going to California to study Scientology," I announced.

"What's Scientology?" she asked suspiciously.

"It's a new science of the mind. It's the psychology of the future. I'm going to train to become an auditor, a new kind of counselor. I'll be able to really help people."

She arrived the following day and begged me to finish the semester before going West. "What kind of school is Scientology, anyway? I've never heard of it, and neither has your father. Are you sure it's accredited?"

"Mom," I said, feeling slightly annoyed by her lack of enthusiasm, "what does it matter if it's not accredited? It's new. It's light-years ahead of traditional psychology." I heard that phrase at the center. "I'll be able to really help people. That's all I ever wanted."

Unconvinced but seeing I couldn't be dissuaded, she helped me load my meager belongings into the back of the station wagon. "We'll keep everything for you in the basement until you return."

As she drove off, I looked at my empty apartment and thought, *There's no turning back now. LA, here I come.*

The airplane's wheels touched down, jolting me back into the present. I retrieved my one small suitcase and asked directions to a bus going to Los Angeles. Inside my purse was a slip of paper with the words *820 S. Burlington Street. Celebrity Center. Antonio Ferraro* on it.

I probably looked like any other student in the late sixties in my Indian-print dress, leather sandals, and apple-seed necklace. One hour and a crowded bus ride later, I stood outside a low wooden building on the corner of Burlington and Eighth Streets in downtown Los Angeles, in the MacArthur Park district.

The large sign on the building read *Welcome to Celebrity Center.* A smaller sign on the door read, *A Center for Artists. Church of Scientology.*

I'd been told that the main Scientology center, the Los Angeles Org, was a few blocks away on Ninth Street, but the Celebrity Center was a special center that catered to artists and celebrities in the motion-picture business. Because of my musical abilities, I'd been referred there.

The front door was open. I walked in and was immediately greeted by a short, older woman with clear blue eyes and an eager smile.

"Hello, Dear," she said, putting her hand on my arm in a friendly gesture. "May I help you?"

"I'm supposed to ask for Antonio. I just arrived from Ann Arbor." I gave Rita's name.

"Oh, yes. We've been expecting you. I'm so glad you're here. Come. Let's find Antonio and get you started."

I followed her into a large room just behind the reception area. It was slightly dark, and my eyes took a moment to adjust.

There were several long rows of tables with about twelve people sitting at them, obviously absorbed in study. Some quietly conversed in pairs as they worked.

I was immediately struck by how quiet the room was, like a library. The only sounds were the low murmur of voices and the soft rustle of paper.

A woman in a white uniform slowly circled the tables, studying the students. She occasionally wrote something on the clipboard she carried, then handed a pink sheet to one of the students.

At the front of the room was an older man at a desk piled with manila folders. The sign on the desk read *Registrar*. The older woman, who introduced herself as Aileen, led me to the desk.

"This is Antonio." She smiled. "Antonio, this is Margery. She's just come from Michigan to do some training with us. I know you'll help her become oriented."

She took my hand. "We'll talk later. The most important thing is for you to get started on course." She averted her intense gaze and looked at Antonio with a knowing smile. He nodded, looked at me, and pointed toward a chair at his desk.

"Welcome." He smiled broadly. "Welcome to Scientology, the Road to Total Freedom."

I would hear that phrase often in the coming years.

He gestured toward the classroom. "This is our course room. This is where we teach Dianetics and where you'll learn to become an auditor." He paused and regarded me as if wondering whether to reveal a secret. "Miracles happen here every day. Miracles. You'll see."

I looked back at the room. To the side of the long tables were students in pairs, sitting in chairs facing each other and staring wordlessly into each other's eyes.

"What are they doing?" I asked.

"They're doing TR Zero. TR stands for Training Routine. It's one of the drills in the Dianetics course. It improves eye contact and your confront as an auditor."

"Confront?" I'd never heard that word used as a noun before.

"That means the ability of the auditor to accept whatever the preclear says or does in the auditing session without any reaction from his own case."

"Case?"

"Yes. Case is a word we use for the preclear's reactive mind. It's also called a bank. When the person's reactive mind or bank is restimulated, it means he's keyed in or banky."

I looked at him and laughed. "Did I just land on another planet? I feel like I'm learning a new language."

"That's because Scientology is different from any other subject. We use new words so people studying our courses don't get Scientology confused with ideas in other subjects, like psychology."

"What are those people doing?" I pointed to a small table where two people were making small clay figures.

"That's the clay table. In all your courses here, you'll be asked to demonstrate the concepts you're learning in clay. You have to actually show the ideas in clay. That's to add mass to the significance of the written words. Hubbard found that people become sleepy when they read for long periods. When you add mass to their learning, either through practical drills or demonstrating in clay, the people become more alert and can study longer."

At another table, I saw a student with headphones listening to a tape recording. He chuckled occasionally as he listened.

I looked back at Antonio. "This is different from any classroom I've ever seen. It's not like school at all."

"You're in for many surprises in Scientology." He beamed at me. "Your life will never be the same again."

"Everyone keeps saying that." I surveyed the strange classroom. "So, Antonio, what should I do to get started?"

He pulled out a long piece of paper printed with green ink. "This is a routing form." He began filling it out. "We'll just get you routed onto course."

After several routine questions, he asked, "How much money did you bring with you?"

"Five hundred dollars. Maybe a little more."

"That's great. That's exactly the cost of the Dianetics course." He looked at me happily. "You'll be able to get started right away."

"I thought the first course was the Communication Course." In Ann Arbor, I was told my first course would cost only fifty dollars.

"Yes, many people start with that, but in your case, you can go directly to the Dianetics Course. That'll save you some money. All the materials from the Communication Course are included in the Dianetics Course, so you won't lose anything. I can see that you have too much awareness for the Communication Course, anyway. You're ready for Dianetics."

I accepted his explanation, but there was a problem. "What'll I do about a place to stay and a job? This is all the money I have."

"That's no problem," he assured me. "We'll find a place next door for you to stay. Right now, all you have to worry about is being on course. Everything will be taken care of."

I handed him my total savings. After I signed the routing form in several places, Antonio led me to the woman in the white uniform.

"This is the course supervisor," he said, introducing me. "She'll give you your course pack. If you have any questions, she's the person to ask. We'll have time to talk again later."

With none of the smiling warmth of Antonio or Aileen, the Course Supervisor stared at me with an expressionless face. "Sit over there." She motioned me to an empty seat. "I'll get you your pack."

A minute later, she handed me a two-inch-thick bound legal-sized packet with the word DIANETICS printed in red ink

The first few pages of the pack were labeled *CHECKSHEET*. Each item of the checksheet was numbered, and there were spaces after each one that were obviously to be initialed after the item was read. Some of the lines had a star, with the explanation that all such items were to be *star-rated* by another student. I would be quizzed on these items by another student, who then had to initial my sheet.

As I looked through the pack, I noticed some of the pages were printed in green ink. At the top, they were labeled *HCO POLICY LETTER*. Farther on in the pack were sheets printed in red and labeled *HCO BULLETIN*. At the top of all the pages were the words *HUBBARD COMMUNICATIONS OFFICE, Saint Hill Manor, East Grinstead, Sussex*.

I turn to the first page after the checksheet, a green page with the title, *The Aims of Scientology*.

> A civilization without insanity, without criminals, and without war, where the able can prosper and honest beings can have rights, and where Man is free to rise to greater heights, are the aims of Scientology.
>
> First announced to an enturbulated world fifteen years ago, these aims are well within the grasp of our technology.
>
> Nonpolitical in nature, Scientology welcomes any individual of any creed, race, or nation.
>
> Your help is acceptable to us.
>
> Our help is yours.

At the bottom was the signature of L. Ron Hubbard.

That sounds really great, I thought, initialing my checksheet and turning the page.

Next, I started reading Hubbard's biography. He was born in Nebraska in 1911 and was raised on his grandfather's cattle ranch in Montana. He could ride before he could walk. As a teenager, he spent several years traveling in Asia, studying with lama priests and "other warlike people."

Later, he enrolled at George Washington University and was a member of the first course in nuclear physics. He later led an expedition into Central America to study savage cultures.

He was crippled and blinded at the end of World War II, but he cured himself by applying his discoveries about the mind. Although twice pronounced dead, he was later given a perfect bill of health.

With the publication of *Dianetics, the Modern Science of Mental Health,* Scientology was established as a worldwide organization. *Scientology is the most vital movement on earth today. Every week, thousands of new people are introduced to its great benefits.*

The biography concluded, *The long-sought bridge to total freedom for Mankind was complete.*

Next, I read an essay in green ink titled *My Philosophy,* by L. Ron Hubbard.

> I like to help others and count it as my greatest pleasure in life to see a person free himself of the shadows which darken his days....
>
> I have lived no cloistered life and hold in contempt the wise man who has not lived; the scholar who will not share....
>
> There have been many wiser men than I, but few have traveled as much road....
>
> I have seen life from the top down and from the bottom up. I know how it looks both ways. And I know that there is wisdom and that there is hope....
>
> No man has any monopoly upon the wisdom of this universe. It belongs to those who can use it to help themselves and others.
>
> If things were a little better known and understood, we would all lead happier lives.

> And there is a way to know them, and there is a way to freedom.
>
> The old must give way to the new, falsehood must be exposed by truth, and truth, though fought, always in the end prevails.

Again, at the bottom, was Hubbard's signature.

The next essay was entitled *Safeguarding Technology*. In it, Hubbard stated:

> In 50,000 years of history on this planet alone, Man never evolved a workable system. It is doubtful if, in foreseeable history, he will ever evolve another.
>
> Man is caught in a huge and complex labyrinth. To get out of it requires that he follow the closely taped path of Scientology.
>
> It has taken me a third of a century in this lifetime to tape this route out....
>
> Scientology is the only workable system Man has. It has already taken people toward higher IQs, better lives, and all that. No other system has. So realize it has no competitor....
>
> Don't let your party down. By whatever means, keep them on the route. And they'll be free. If you don't, they won't.

In my mind, I almost heard a band playing. Patriotism I never knew I possessed stirred inside me. *At last, after 18 depressing years of frustration and failure, maybe I've finally found the winning team.*

The next essay was more intense and hinted of danger.

> When somebody enrolls, consider he or she has joined up for the duration of the universe—never permit an open-minded approach. If they're going to quit, let them quit fast. If they enrolled, they're aboard, and if they're aboard, they're here on the same terms as the rest of us—win or die in the attempt.

As I read to the end of the policy letter, I came to a paragraph I had to read twice. Did it say what I think it said?

> We're not playing some minor game in Scientology. It isn't cute or something to do for lack of something better.... The whole agonized future of this planet, every Man, Woman, and Child on it, and your own destiny for the next trillions of years, depends on what you do here and now with and in Scientology.

Wow, I thought. *Heavy.* That was more than I expected. Really, what *had* I expected?

I looked around the room at the other students, who were quietly studying. I suddenly felt I not only arrived in a different city, but in a different world.

Whatever had been important to me before paled in comparison with what I was discovering on these pages. I was being led into a new world, with new ideas, new words, new people, and new priorities.

In one day, my priorities shifted from the mundane unimportance of my barren life as a college student to the profound ideals I was discovering in these pages. It was almost scary. In reading Hubbard's words, I felt a challenge to go beyond anything I had ever expected of myself or imagined myself capable of. Here was a chance to be and do something heroic.

How often, I wondered, *does a person have a chance like this, to make a universal difference in life?*

Good-bye, old life, I thought.

Somehow, after reading just those few pages, I knew I wouldn't be returning to college soon. Instead, I walked eagerly and trustingly into the world of Scientology, without so much as a backward look. If this was the ship, called Scientology, I was aboard.

CHAPTER FOUR

Flunk for Laughing! Start!

Just as I was finishing the last policy letter in the first section of my checksheet, the Course Supervisor called out in a loud voice, "That's it. Afternoon break."

Immediately, chairs were pushed back and study packs closed, as everyone filed out the front door into the parking lot. A long, square log bordering a small garden by the front door served as a bench for the students during the break. Several lit up cigarettes.

I noticed a girl about my own age sitting by herself. "Hi. I'm Margery. I just started the course this afternoon."

"Hi. Welcome. I'm Kris." She held out her hand to shake. "What do you think so far?"

"It's pretty wild. This is different from anything I've ever done before. I guess I'm still wondering if it's all real. Maybe I'm just having a very strange dream." I laughed, as I turned up the sleeves of my dress to take advantage of the hot California sun.

"Oh, it's real all right. I wondered at the beginning, too, but the auditing really works. That's what convinced me. I've had so many wins from auditing. Now I just want to get up the bridge and go OT. That's where it's at." She stared abstractedly into the distance for a few seconds. "How did you get in, anyway?"

"A friend at school in Michigan. Everything's happened so fast. If you had told me a week ago that I'd be dropping out of school and coming to California, I would've thought you were crazy, but here I am." I shook my head as she offered me a cigarette. "How about you? How did you get in?"

"My whole family is in. My brother got in first, then my parents. Now my parents are in the Sea Org. They're on the ship. My brother's an auditor at the Org." She pointed vaguely southwest. "I would've joined the Sea Org, too. It would be cool to be on the ship with Ron, but I have a small part in a film, so I can't leave right now."

"Ron?" I was puzzled by the name.

"Ron Hubbard. He likes us to call him Ron. He's neat. He really cares about everyone. Wait till you listen to his tapes. He's funny, but he's a genius who figured out how the mind works. No one else for thousands of years has been able to figure it out." She looked at me with her eyes sparkling.

"Have you ever met him?"

"No, but I'd give anything just to say hello to him once. He pretty much stays on the ship. I'm so jealous of my parents. They get to work with him every day. I could've gone on the ship, but I want to become a famous actress first. That's the best way I can help with the third dynamic, by getting my acting into power."

"Third dynamic?"

The question was just out of my mouth when I heard a stern voice say, "That's it. End of break. Let's get back on course. I want to see some stats this afternoon." The uniformed Course Supervisor stood in the doorway looking very military, with a red lanyard around her neck and a whistle attached. I waited for her to use it, but she didn't.

The students quickly followed her into the course room. As soon as everyone was seated, the supervisor called out, "All right. Start!" The classroom was immediately quiet again.

I looked at my checksheet. The next section was called Training Drills. According to the instructions, I needed a twin to do the drills.

I went up to the Supervisor, who looked around the room. "OK. George needs to do TRs. Go have a seat, and I'll get him." She pointed to pairs of chairs in the back of the room.

A minute later, an older man approached and stretched out his hand. "Hi," he said warmly. "I'm George. I hear you need to do TRs."

"I guess." I hesitated. "I've never done them before."

"That's OK. Let's read the bulletin." He opened his pack to the same page I was on.

> TR 0 Confronting. Purpose: To train student to confront a preclear with auditing only or with nothing. Training Stress: Have student and coach sit facing each other, neither making any conversation or effort to be interesting. Have them sit and look at each other and say and do nothing for some hours. Students must not speak, fidget, giggle, or be embarrassed....

"All right." George looked at me pleasantly. "I'll be the coach. We do this for two hours. Get comfortable."

I adjusted my position in the chair and put my hands on my lap.

"Ready?" George sat in a similar position directly across from me. Our knees were almost touching.

I nodded.

"OK, start!"

I looked into George's eyes, wondering what would happen. He looked back with a flawless, unblinking stare. I blinked.

"Flunk for blinking. Start!" he said sternly.

"You mean I can't even blink?" I asked incredulously.

"Flunk for talking! Start!" He maintained his perfect stare into my eyes.

I tried to return the same perfect stare he gave me. My mouth began to quiver.

"Flunk for moving your mouth. Start!" He was merciless.

All right, I thought. *This is serious.* Then I thought of something. "George, wait a minute. If I flunk, does that mean we have to start the two hours over again?"

"That's it." He temporarily ended the drill and smiled. "Right. The two hours start over again every time I say, 'Start.'

When you can do TR 0 flawlessly for two hours, we're finished with the drill."

Before I could ask anything else, he resumed his staring and commanded, "Flunk for talking. Start!" and we were off again.

I tried as hard as I could not to blink. Soon, tears welled up in my eyes. They burned from the salty liquid, but I forced myself not to blink. George continued his seemingly effortless, blinkless stare.

As I stared into his eyes, I began to see an aura of colors flowing in streams around his head. Then the colors expanded into the whole room. I watched with awe, as the room became filled with flowing color.

Meanwhile, my pain increased. Tears ran down my cheeks. Inside, I cried with pain, but stubbornness competed with the pain. *If he can do it,* I thought with determination, *then I can, too.* I felt pain in my whole body. I was suddenly conscious of the chair, and it felt painful against my skin. I wanted desperately to move and ease the pain of the chair against the pressure points of my body. It was torture.

My body felt contorted out of shape. The flowing colors in the room became even more vivid. Feeling strangely dizzy, I wondered if I would pass out. I was lightheaded, almost like I felt once at the dentist when I was given gas before having a tooth extracted.

How much time passed? I continued my stare, though I wanted to look at my watch. I wondered how we would know when two hours passed. The thought of having to sit there until the Supervisor called the dinner break wasn't pleasant.

The excruciating pain at the point where my hipbones met the chair faded, and I felt as if I were expanding like a balloon to fill the entire room.

Suddenly, I had a rush of euphoria. I was floating, looking down at everyone from a thousand points all over the room. It was better than anything I ever experienced with marijuana.

Far out, I thought, realizing the pain was gone. *I could sit like this for a thousand years.* I enjoyed the expansive high. The colors were gone. Instead, I saw the room with crystal clarity and felt unaccustomed serenity. *I could stay like this forever,* I thought.

George reached forward and tapped my shoulder. "That's it," he said quietly. "You just passed TR 0."

"Wow. I don't know if I can even stand up. I feel like I've been blasted out of my head."

"Exactly." He smiled at me. "Congratulations. Most people don't do that well the first time. I can see that you'll be an excellent student."

I tried moving my head. I still felt I was located at some remote point from my body, making motion difficult. I tried to stand and stretch, but I felt dizzy, as if I were moving my body by remote control.

George looked at his watch. "We don't have any time to do any more before dinner. Why don't we continue after dinner? That'll give you some time to enjoy your win from TR 0." He seemed to understand I was still trying to regain control of my body. "Don't worry. You're probably feeling a bit exterior. It takes a little getting used to. I'll see you here after dinner."

I opened my pack and looked at the next drill.

> TR 0 Bullbait. Purpose: To train student to confront a preclear with auditing or with nothing. The whole idea is to get the student able to BE there comfortably in a position three feet in front of the preclear without being thrown off, distracted, or reacting in any way to what the preclear says or does.
>
> Training Stress: After the student has passed TR 0 and he can just BE there comfortably, "bull baiting" can begin. Anything added to BEING THERE is sharply flunked by the coach. The coach may say anything or do anything except

leave the chair. The student's "buttons" can
be found and tromped on hard.

I read it over a second time, but I still didn't understand what we were supposed to do. I decided to ask the Supervisor.

"Excuse me. I don't understand this drill. Can you explain it to me?"

She looked at me with disapproval. "What word don't you understand?" she asked coldly.

"What word?"

"Yes. According to the tech, if you don't understand something in the materials, then it means you've gone past a word you didn't understand. You need to find your word and look it up." She handed me a dictionary from the table.

Confused, I decided to take her advice and reread the passage. I looked up the word *baited.* Maybe that was it. I turned to the dictionary.

Bait, I read, *3. To tease or goad, especially so as to provoke a reaction.*

That sounded right. I read the passage again, and it made a little more sense.

The Supervisor called the dinner break. I went over to Antonio, who was still seated at his desk.

"How was your course?" Antonio smiled at me. "I heard you did TR 0 like a pro. That means you'll make an excellent auditor." He didn't give me a chance to reply. "I suppose I should show you to your accommodations." He got up from the desk and led me to the front door. We walked around the corner to a large blue house directly behind the center.

"This is our staff house," he explained, as we approached the house. "You'll be staying here until we can find you permanent accommodations."

"But how am I going to pay for it? What about food? I don't have any more money."

"You can pay us back by becoming a top-notch auditor." He smiled. "You'll be eating with us in the staff dining room. Come, I'll show you."

First, he took me to a small room with three beds just off the hall in the front of the house. "I think this one is unoccupied." He pointed to the bed just inside the door.

I put my suitcase under the bed.

"Let's go eat."

We walked back to the dining room where Aileen and six or seven other people were already eating. I was told to take a plate and help myself. The food was served family style. I hadn't eaten on the plane, so I was famished, and I was beginning to feel the fatigue of a long day participating in unfamiliar events.

Listening to conversation at the table, I realized I didn't understand much of what they were saying. It really seemed like a different language. Many of the words were familiar, but they were using them in ways I'd never heard them used before.

"This is really an upstat dinner," Aileen said. "The cook must be in power."

"Yeah." A blond-haired man in a navy-blue uniform with gold braid laughed. "After he got over his ARC break about three unexpected people for dinner." He looked at me. "Is this a new PC?" he asked Antonio.

"Yes," Antonio replied. "This is Margery. She's just been selected here. Julie is her Field Staff Member. Her stats are already in affluence after her first day on course."

"Outstanding." The blond man looked at me approvingly. "We need some new blood in Tech."

I was too busy eating to ask questions, so I listened and tried to understand as much of the unusual conversation as I could.

After dinner, I volunteered to help with the dishes.

"No," Aileen answered, taking plates from my hand. "You're not hatted to work in the kitchen. We have a kitchen I/C to take care of everything."

"Hatted? Kitchen I/C?" I thought I'd never learn all the new words.

"I'm sorry." She put her arm on my shoulder. "I keep forgetting that you don't know our words yet. I guess I've been here too long.

"Every job in Scientology is called a post, and for every job, no matter how menial, there is a pack of materials that a person studies to learn or be hatted on that post. For example, Kitchen in Charge is a post, and only when a person has been hatted on that post can he take over the job.

"Anyway," she looked at her watch, "you need to be getting back on course."

We walked back to the center together. I looked at the lush vegetation surrounding the house. "I can't believe it's the end of October. I've never seen so many beautiful flowers. At home, everything is brown this time of year." I admired the bottlebrush bushes lining the sidewalk.

"I guess we take it for granted," Aileen admitted. "I'm usually so busy, I don't take time to notice."

"Do you ever have time off?"

"We have personal time on Saturday morning. That's about all. I don't mind the long hours. I feel honored to be helping Ron. We have a planet to clear, and that's a big job, and there may not be much earth time to do it in."

I remembered the poster on the wall of a house in Ann Arbor. "Why? Do you think something's going to happen?"

"We are the only organization on earth that can prevent a nuclear disaster. Ron says we have about seven years to clear the planet. That's all the time we have. If we fail, then that's it. This planet will no longer exist."

"How can Scientology prevent a nuclear war?"

"By getting everyone on the planet Clear. When people no longer have their reactive minds, they will no longer be interested in petty disputes over territory. There will be no more war. Unless we succeed, this world is doomed. Technology has advanced much faster than man's ability to use that technology in a sane way. That's what happened on this planet thousands of years ago. We tried to prevent a disaster once before, but we failed. We can't afford to fail again."

I walked silently beside her, thinking about what she said. "So there was civilization on the earth in the past, and it was destroyed by atom bombs?"

"Yes, thousands of years ago, before any recorded history that people know about today. You'll find out more about that in your auditing."

We arrived at the center. I went in and took my seat.

"That's it," the Supervisor called. "Start of class."

I met George by the chairs. "I'm not sure what is meant by bull baiting."

"We'll just do it, and you'll see."

We took the same chairs we used that afternoon.

"Get comfortable."

I relaxed in the chair and put my hands in my lap.

"Start!"

I sat and again stared into his eyes. It seemed much easier this time. I began to relax and enjoy the same expansive sensation I experienced earlier.

Suddenly, George leaned forward. "I see what you're up to," he said slyly. "You're trying to seduce me, aren't you? You just think I'm an easy lay."

I stared at him without moving, not sure what to do.

"I know you girls from Michigan." His voice became louder. Students at other tables looked in our direction. "Your reputation has preceded you. I know what you're interested in. It's sex." He said the last word very loudly, his face close to mine.

My eyes were beginning to tear.

"I know all about you. You're just interested in one thing, aren't you? And here I thought you liked me for my mind," he said in disgust.

Some of the students were beginning to smile.

"You're not interested in my mind at all, are you? You just want my body. That's it, isn't it? You just want my body." He leaned over with his face next to mine.

I started to smile, losing my composure because of my embarrassment.

"Flunk for smiling! Start!" he said loudly. "You just want my body, don't you?"

He repeated that phrase a few times. I tried desperately to control my muscles.

"You know what you look like? You look like a hippie. Look at those beads." He took hold of my apple-seed necklace. "You must be a hippie, a trippy hippie. Come on, tell me the truth. Do you like to trip? Did you ever trip and have sex? How do you like it? Sex, I mean. Are you good in bed? I'll bet you are. You Michigan girls are always good in bed."

My eyes were tearing, and I was in excruciating pain. I blinked, and tears flowed down my face.

"Flunk for blinking! Start! I know all about you Michigan girls. Say, what kind of hairstyle is this?" He pulled my hair. "I've seen better hairstyles at the zoo. And those clothes. Really," he said with mock sarcasm. "Couldn't you find something that fits? Don't you want to show off your body? Do you mind if I look at your body?"

I felt humiliated. More tears flowed from my unblinking eyes. My mouth began to twitch.

"Flunk for twitching! Start! So you have a button on your body? Well, we'll just have to work on that. What don't you like about your body? Come on, you can tell me."

I continued staring.

"You know, you could stand to lose some weight. Just a little, though. I don't like girls who are too thin. You have that country look, that wholesome look. Are you wholesome? I'll bet you are. Maybe you've never had sex. Maybe you're a virgin. I've never met a virgin before."

I decided to look at one point on his face and concentrate on that instead of what he was saying. I chose a spot in the middle of his forehead, which made it a little easier.

Suddenly, he clapped his hands in front of my face, and I jumped.

"Flunked for moving! Start!" He clapped his hands again. I didn't move.

He leaned over and blew in my ear. "Did you like that? Did you? I could do it again." He leaned toward me. I followed him with my eyes without moving anything else.

"Very good, Margery. Very good. You're doing very well. You'll make a fine auditor. That's it. You pass TR 0 bullbaited."

I tried to relax my body. Strangely, since I was doing TR 0, I couldn't seem to stop it. No matter how hard I tried, I couldn't blink. My eyes were ready to pop out of my head. I still had the high feeling I had during the exercise. I felt like I was stoned.

George clapped my shoulder. "Don't take it personally. It's just part of the drill. Now it's your turn to bullbait me."

I looked at him in shock. "I can't do that." I looked at him desperately.

"Why not?" He smiled. "It's just part of the drill. Everyone has to do it. It isn't anything personal."

"I know, but I don't want to hurt your feelings."

"That's just the thing. There isn't anything personal about it. It's just part of the training to be an auditor. You're actually doing me a favor by finding my buttons and flattening them. Go ahead. Try it."

"Start!" He sat back and resumed his TR 0.

I swallowed. "All right, Mister. You gave it to me, and I'm going to give it right back to you. Think you can take it?"

His eyebrow moved.

"Flunk for moving your eyebrow. Start! Think you can take it? What kind of man are you, anyway? How could you ask me all those embarrassing questions? Those things are none of your business." I sat there, unable to continue, and started to laugh. "George, I can't do this. I'm not used to it."

He relaxed and smiled. "OK, I guess we've done enough for one day. Your confront will come up. It won't be long before you'll be able to bullbait anyone. That's enough for now."

He shook my hand. "We'll finish the TRs tomorrow. You might like to listen to a tape of Hubbard for the rest of the class tonight."

He showed me where the tapes were kept in a file cabinet in the back of the room and handed me a tape. I plugged in the headphones, wound the tape leader around the take-up reel, and started the tape. I immediately heard a booming voice.

"Welcome to the Saint Hill Special Briefing Course," Hubbard intoned to his invisible audience. "What's the year?" He paused. "AD what?"

"AD 15?" someone asked from the audience. I later learned that Scientologists numbered their years from the date Dianetics was published. AD 15 to a Scientologist would be 1965.

"OK," continued the mellifluous voice. "What planet are we on? Earth? What in the world are we doing on Earth?"

The audience laughed.

Hubbard's voice had a hypnotic effect. He sounded so confident and certain of himself. As I listened, he told spellbinding stories about different things he'd done in his life, anecdotes about his experiences in the circus, as a seaman, as a photographer, and as a pilot. It seemed as if there wasn't anything he hadn't done.

After a while, I found it very difficult to follow his train of thought. Some of the sentences didn't make sense, and I wondered what the point of the tape was. Still, I found myself unable to stop listening. There was something about his voice that was compelling. Maybe it was just the fact that he sounded more sure of himself than anyone I ever heard before. Even on tape, he exuded the jovial confidence of a man who had life firmly under control.

"Life is just a game," he instructed his audience, "not to be taken seriously. Seriousness equals mass."

That's a new way of looking at it, I mused.

The day's events were beginning to catch up with me. I found myself yawning. The Supervisor came over to me.

"Take off the headphones," she commanded with her expressionless face.

"Find your MU," she said tersely.

"My MU?" I asked with a tired voice.

"Yes. Your misunderstood word. The only reason a person yawns when studying is because of a misunderstood word. You'll have to find your word, then go back earlier in the tape and listen to it again."

"I think I'm just tired." I looked up at her. "It's been a very long day."

"Don't Q and A." She sounded annoyed. "According to the tech, the only reason a person yawns while studying is because of an MU. The tech is never wrong, so find your MU. That's an order."

"OK," I answered meekly. I went to find a dictionary. I saw a Scientology dictionary lying on the table and looked up the expression *Q and A.*

> Q and A means question-and-answer.
> It means one did not get an answer to
> his question. It also means not getting
> compliance with an order....

I rewound the tape and started again. Did I really have a misunderstood word? Couldn't I just be tired? I wondered about her statement, "The tech is never wrong." Something about that bothered me, but I wasn't sure what it was. I returned to listening to the tape, trying to locate a word I hadn't understood.

Soon, however, it was 10:30, and I heard, "That's it. End of class. Let's gather around to report our wins."

Chairs scraped against the floor, as everyone squeezed in around one table.

"All right," the Supervisor stood stiffly in front of us. "Who had a win today?"

"I did," a student volunteered. I looked over at a young, slender boy sitting across from me. "I was auditing a PC (preclear), and he totally keyed out. I really cognited today that this really does work, and I can actually help people. I just feel really good about the tech, and I'm grateful to Ron for giving it to us."

The rest of the class applauded.

"Yeah," another student said, "I did a touch assist today, and the PC's migraine headache just blew. This stuff is dynamite."

There was more applause.

"My PC finally ran past lives today, and she had a big win," a third student volunteered. "I can't wait to do more sessions."

The Supervisor interrupted. "We have a new student today. This is Margery, from Michigan. Would you like to share your wins with us tonight?"

Everyone looked at me expectantly.

"Well, everything is all so new. I'm not really sure. I guess you could say I keyed out when I did TR 0. I didn't think I'd be able to do it, but toward the end, I felt like I could sit there forever. I felt really good at the end," I volunteered, not wanting to let them down. I felt relieved when they applauded.

I hadn't even had time to think about everything that happened during the day. When did the day begin? I tried to remember. That morning in Michigan seemed like an event from the remote past.

A few other students shared their wins, then we were dismissed. I walked back to the house looking up at the bright stars in the western sky. Was it possible that I was still living in the same world, and these were the same stars shining that night in faraway Michigan skies? Already, that world seemed to be fading into the distant past. This was a different world entirely. I felt myself starting to become a different person.

Walking back to the house, I felt as if I could almost touch the sky. The heady euphoria from the TRs was still with me.

The Road to Total Freedom, I thought, looking up at the starry sky. I wondered where that road would lead me.

CHAPTER FIVE

Do Fish Swim? Do Birds Fly?

I was in a strange city in which the buildings were all in a monotonous shade of gray. I stood in the middle of a wide street, as hundreds of people ran past, shouting at me and motioning me to follow. I sensed danger. Everyone seemed to be running toward an opening at the side of the street that resembled the entrance to a subway station. As I ran down into the dark opening, a door closed heavily behind me.

In the darkness, I saw people huddled together, some crying, some silent. Suddenly, I understood it was a bomb shelter. I was in a city of the future. The faces around me mirrored the terror I felt inside.

Suddenly, I felt the impact of something hitting the ground above us with tremendous force. The earth shook violently. People began screaming, as panic spread. I knew there was no hope. The earth shook crazily, as all life above us was destroyed.

I opened my eyes. Sunlight streamed through the front windows. *Oh,* I thought with relief, *it was just a dream.*

Then I realized that the earth really was shaking. The pictures on the opposite wall swayed back and forth. "What in the world?" I asked.

On the other side of the room, a man with deep-blue eyes and a dark suntan watched me with obvious interest. He wore a white uniform with gold braid hanging from the shoulder. He sat on his cot, putting on his shoes.

"Don't worry. It's only a tremor." He seemed oblivious to the shaking. "We get them all the time."

I didn't say anything but lay there clutching my sheet and waiting for the shaking to stop. Finally, it did.

"I never felt anything like that before." I tried not to let my voice reflect my panic. "If that's just a tremor, I'd hate to be in a real one."

I looked curiously at my roommate. The room had been empty when I came back from class the previous night. I fell into an exhausted sleep and didn't remember anyone coming into the room during the night. The third bed also looked like it had been slept in.

"Sea Org members must not get much sleep," I commented. "I didn't hear you come in during the night."

He looked over and smiled. "We can't be thinking about sleep when there's a planet to clear," he said. "We can catch up on sleep later. Ron says that every minute of time is like a gold coin that we have to spend. How we spend them may very well determine the fate of the Earth."

He looked over at me challengingly, and I felt guilty for being in bed.

"What time is it, anyway?" I didn't see a clock in the room.

"It's about 0800. Aren't you supposed to be on course?"

"Oh, no! I'm late!" I wailed. Grabbing my clothes, I ran to the bathroom down the hall. Within seconds, I was sprinting toward the center. There was no time for coffee that morning. I had a second to glance appreciatively at the warm morning sun, already high in the sky.

I walked into the course room and looked around for George. He was busy giving a checkout to one of the other students. As I looked in his direction, trying to get his attention, I heard a voice behind me.

"Miss Wakefield, you're late."

It was more accusation than observation. I turned and looked into the steely eyes of the Supervisor.

"I'm afraid you have to go to Ethics." She handed me a pink sheet of paper on which she had written, *Late for class. To Ethics for handling.*

"Ethics?" I looked to her for an explanation.

"Ethics. They're in the back. You'll see the sign on the door." She pointed down the hall to an office in the back.

Obediently, I headed down the hall and knocked on the half-open door with a sign that read, *Ethics. Master at Arms.*

"Come in." The voice sounded like a child's.

Peering into the room, I saw a young, teenage boy seated at a desk behind an E-meter. "Well? What is it?" He looked at me coldly.

"I was late for course." I handed him the pink sheet. "I'm afraid I overslept. I was extremely exhausted last night."

"Do you have some counter-intention to being on course?" He looked at me accusingly.

"Counter-intention?"

He handed me a Scientology dictionary. "Look it up."

I took the dictionary and quickly turned to the Cs. *Counter-intention. A determination to follow a goal which is in direct conflict with those known to be the goals of the group.*

"You need to locate your counter-intention that caused you to be late for course," he said matter-of-factly.

"Well, I think it was just that no one woke me up. I don't have an alarm clock. I'd buy one, but I spent all my money on the course." I looked at him helplessly. Why was I feeling guilty?

"I'd like to indicate that you are in a condition of danger." He looked at me coldly.

Why was I feeling so defensive around this kid? He couldn't be older than thirteen or fourteen, yet he had the demeanor of someone much older. He spoke with the authority of an adult accustomed to commanding others.

"What is a condition of danger?" I felt more and more insecure.

"Here." He handed me a set of papers in red ink, stapled together, with the title, *Conditions*. "Go back in the course room and star-rate this HCOB."

I guessed that HCOB stood for Hubbard Communications Office Bulletin, which was printed at the top of the first page.

"When you finish that, come back and see me. Make sure you look up your misunderstood words." He looked down at his work, and I realized I was dismissed.

I returned to the course room and began to read through the bulletin he gave me. *Conditions. A condition is an operating state, and oddly enough in the physical universe, there are several formulas connected with these operating states.*

There was a list of twelve conditions—Power, Power Change, Affluence, Normal Operation, Emergency, Danger, Nonexistence, Liability, Doubt, Enemy, Treason, and Confusion.

Each condition had a formula. The formulas were to be applied one step at a time, until the entire formula was completed, at which time the person could apply to be upgraded to the next-higher condition.

The formula for the condition of Confusion, the lowest condition, was, *Find Out Where You Are.*

I wonder what that means? I looked carefully through the sentence. I understood all the words, but it still didn't make any sense. I decided not to ask and read the next one.

> Treason is defined as betrayal after trust.
> The formula for the condition of treason is
> Find Out Who You Are.
>
> When a person is an avowed and knowing enemy of an individual, a group, a project, or organization, a condition of Enemy exists. The formula for the condition of Enemy is just one step—Find Out Who You Really Are.

The next formula was more complex.

> When one cannot make up one's mind as to an individual, a group, organization, or project, a condition of Doubt exists. The formula is:
>
> Inform oneself honestly of the actual intentions and activities of the individual, group, project, or organization, brushing aside all bias and rumor.
>
> Examine the statistics of the individual, group, project, or organization.
>
> Decide on the basis of "the greatest good for the greatest number of dynamics" whether or not it should be attacked, harmed, suppressed, or helped.

Then, after one examines the statistics of the group one currently belonged to, one would, *Join or remain in or befriend the one that progresses toward the greatest number of dynamics and announce it publicly to both sides.*

The word *Dynamics* was being used in a new and unfamiliar context. I picked up the Scientology dictionary.

> There could be said to be eight urges in life. These we call dynamics. These are motives or motivations. We call them the eight dynamics.
>
> The first dynamic is the urge toward existence as oneself. Here we have individuality expressed fully. This can be called the self-dynamic.
>
> The second dynamic is the urge toward

existence as a sexual or bisexual activity.

I blinked. Had I read that right? I looked again. Yes, that's what it said.

> This dynamic actually has two divisions. Second dynamic (a) is the sexual act itself, and the second dynamic (b) is the family unit, including the rearing of children. This can be called the sex dynamic.
>
> The third dynamic is the urge toward existence in groups of individuals. The school, the society, the town, the nation are each part of the third dynamic, and each one is a third dynamic. This is also called the group dynamic.
>
> The fourth dynamic is the urge toward existence as mankind. Whereas the white race would be considered a third dynamic, all the races would be considered the fourth dynamic. This can be called the mankind dynamic.
>
> The fifth dynamic is the urge toward existence of the animal kingdom. This includes all living things whether animal or vegetable. The fish in the sea, the beasts of the field or the forest, grass, trees, flowers, or anything directly and intimately motivated by life. This could be called the animal dynamic.
>
> The sixth dynamic is the urge toward existence as the physical universe. The physical universe is composed of matter, energy, space, and time. In Scientology, we take the first letter of these words and

> coin a word, *MEST*. This can be called the universe dynamic.
>
> The seventh dynamic is the urge toward existence as or of spirits. Anything spiritual, with or without identity, would come under the heading of the seventh dynamic. This could be called the spiritual dynamic.
>
> The eighth dynamic is the urge toward existence as infinity. This is also identified as the Supreme Being. It is carefully observed here that the science of Scientology does not intrude into the dynamic of the Supreme Being. This can be called the infinity or God dynamic.

I finished reading the lengthy explanation. *This is a new way of categorizing and thinking about life,* I thought. *All right. I can handle that.*

I felt relieved to know that Scientology believed in God. I would find out much more about that later in my Scientology career.

I returned to reading about Conditions. The next one was Liability, for which the formula was:

> Decide who are one's friends.
>
> Deliver an effective blow to the enemies of the group one has been pretending to be part of despite personal danger.
>
> Make up the damage one has done by personal contribution far beyond the ordinary demands of a group member.
>
> Apply for reentry to the group by asking the

permission of each member of it to rejoin and rejoining only by majority permission.

The formula for Nonexistence was simpler:

Find a comm (communication) line.
Make yourself known.
Discover what's needed or wanted.
Do, produce, and/or present it.

I wanted to yawn, but I looked warily at the Supervisor circling the tables and decided to suppress it.

Next, I read through the Danger Formula, the one that apparently applied to me.

Bypass habits or normal routines.

Handle the situation and any danger in it.

Assign self a danger condition.

Get in your own personal ethics by finding what you are doing that is out-ethics and use self-discipline to correct it and get honest and straight.

Reorganize your life, so the dangerous situation is not continually happening to you.

Formulate and adopt firm policy that will hereafter detect and prevent the same situation from continuing to occur.

What I have to do, I thought, *is simply get someone to wake me up in the morning, so this doesn't happen again. That's easy enough.*

I read through the Conditions bulletin again, trying to grasp the material. According to the theory, if I successfully applied the formula for the condition I was in, which was Danger, then I should be able to move up to the next-higher condition. For me, that would be Emergency. Part of the Emergency Formula had to do with changing your operating basis.

> You have got to stiffen discipline or stiffen ethics, because life itself is going to discipline the individual.

That meant I would have to become very disciplined about getting to class on time, I realized. That was no problem.

Once out of Emergency, I would be safely in Normal Operation. I sighed. I didn't realize that oversleeping was so complicated. I would be sure not to do it again if I could help it.

I finished reading the policy, then went to George and asked him to check me out. He did, and I passed easily. I was ready to return to the young dictator in Ethics.

He looked up as I entered. "Did you apply the correct formula?" he asked stiffly.

"I think so." I looked down at him awkwardly. "Mostly, I have to find someone to wake me up every morning."

"Make sure it doesn't happen again, or you'll find yourself in Liability. OK. You can return to course." He initialed the pink sheet and handed it back to me. "Take this back to your Course Supervisor."

"Let me ask you a question. These conditions—what do you use them for? Are they just used on the course?"

He looked at me condescendingly. "The Ethics conditions are one of the greatest gifts we have from Ron. A Scientologist uses the conditions in every area of his life. Every area. You can apply the conditions to everything you do. If you think about it, no matter what you do, you're always in one of the conditions. The trick is to always know which one you're in and then apply the correct formula. If you do that, you can never lose."

"Thanks," I said, grateful for such wisdom from one so young. That was a different way of looking at life. I would have to give it some thought. I was beginning to feel like I didn't know anything, and I had a lot to learn. Scientology was indeed complex.

I returned to course and handed the pink sheet to the Supervisor. She nodded, and I returned to my seat.

"Ready for more TRs?"

I looked up and saw George standing beside me.

"Sure," I replied, eager to progress on the course.

We return to the chairs in the back. To my surprise, he handed me a copy of the book *Alice in Wonderland*. I opened the Training Routines bulletin we used the day before.

> Training Routine 1. Dear Alice. Purpose: To train the student to deliver a command newly and in a new unit of time to a preclear without flinching or trying to overwhelm or using a via. Commands: A phrase (with the "he saids" omitted) is picked out of the book *Alice in Wonderland* and read to the coach. It is repeated until the coach is satisfied it arrived where he is.

"All right." George looked at me brightly. "Start!"

I opened the book and selected a phrase. Then I looked at George and said to him clearly, "Would you tell me please why you are painting those roses?" He was doing TR 0 again, staring intently into my eyes with his serene, unblinking gaze.

"Good," he answered. "Try another one."

"OK." I turned to another page. "It's my opinion that you never think at all," I said, returning his stare. Why did I feel like such a robot? Was that really the way I was supposed to talk to people? It didn't feel natural. I decided to just do the drills and ask questions later.

In the next drill, George read statements out of the book, and I had to acknowledge what he said. *An acknowledgment is a method of controlling preclear communication.*

"It wasn't very civil of you to sit down without being invited," George said.

"OK," I answered self-consciously.

"What you want to do in this drill is to really duplicate what I say to you," George said. "You should be able to repeat the phrase to me verbatim. Let your acknowledgment really tell me that you heard me. Like this. Fine! All right! Thank you!"

I tried again, this time with more confidence.

"I never saw such a house for getting in the way," George said.

"All right," I replied firmly.

"Good. What did I say?"

"I never saw such a house for getting in the way," I repeated.

After a few more practice rounds, we went to the next drill, TR 3, which was supposed to teach me to ask a question, get an answer, and acknowledge the answer in *one unit of time,* The questions were, "Do fish swim?" and, "Do birds fly?"

"Do fish swim?" I asked George, trying to maintain my TR 0.

"Well, I'd rather talk about birds," he answered.

Following the directions in the bulletin, I said gently, "I'll repeat the auditing question. Do fish swim?"

"Oh, sure. They swim all the time."

"Good." I felt successful.

We practiced that drill and the next one, TR 4, which was the same, except in that one, George was allowed to be even more disruptive.

"Do birds fly?" I asked.

George pretended to be angry and got up out of his chair. "This is stupid. I'm getting out of here." He headed for the door.

Again, following the directions in the bulletin, I physically directed him back to his chair. I had to get an answer to my question by any means. It was up to me to maintain control of the situation.

"Do birds fly?" I asked again.

"Sure. They fly all the time," he said agreeably.

"Great!" I delivered the acknowledgment with gusto.

"All right. Pass on TR 4," George said in approval. "That was fine."

I was ready for the last of the TRs, the upper indoc (indoctrination) TRs. George told me those TRs would train me further to maintain control in a session.

In the first drill, I had to direct George around the room using precise commands and acknowledging him for each action. The commands to be used were:

> Look over at that wall. Thank you.
>
> Walk over to that wall. Thank you.
>
> Touch that wall. Thank you.
>
> Turn around. Thank you.

We did the drill for twenty minutes until I was starting to feel dizzy. For some reason, the repetitive commands made me sleepy.

In the following drill, the commands were the same, but I physically had to guide George through the required motions. That one was easy, so we completed it quickly.

The next TR was called *Tone 40 on an Object*. That was a curious drill. The Scientology dictionary explained that Tone 40 was *a positive postulate with no counter thought expected, anticipated, or anything else. That is, total control.*

George sat beside me and put an ashtray in the chair across from me. I read the instructions in the bulletin. Taking the ashtray in my hands, I shouted in my loud-as-possible voice, "Stand up!" I raised the ashtray off the chair and held it in midair. "Thank you," I acknowledged the ashtray. "Sit down on that chair!" I shouted, lowering the ashtray back to the chair. "Thank you!" I shouted again.

"Not loud enough," George said. "I don't feel your total intention. Theoretically, if you do this drill with complete Tone 40, the ashtray will rise by itself off the table. When you give the commands, you can have no other intention than the commands. You're still somewhat self-conscious."

He was right about that. I couldn't believe I was sitting there yelling at an ashtray. If I had to do it, I was determined to do it well.

I yelled even louder, "Stand up!" and raised the ashtray off the table. "Sit down on that chair!" My voice was getting hoarse. I lowered the ashtray and looked at George triumphantly. "How was that?"

"If I had been that ashtray, I would've jumped off the chair." He laughed. "OK. Pass."

The last TR, TR 9, was called *Tone 40 on a Person,* and was similar to the previous drill except that I was to scream the commands at a person. I was to deliver the commands with total Tone 40, giving the other person no choice but to obey. I could use physical means to guide him, if necessary.

"Walk over to that wall!" I yelled at George.

He just stood there. "I didn't feel Tone 40. Try it again."

"Walk over to that wall!" I screamed, my face red with effort. I guided him with my hands. He moved to the wall. "Thank you!"

"Turn around!" I screamed, trying to channel my complete concentration into the command.

"Thank you!" I began to get a headache.

"Sit down in the chair!" I screamed again, my voice getting raspy. "Thank you!"

We continued for a few more commands, then George mercifully gave me a pass on the drill. We ended just in time for lunch.

"You're making splendid progress," George said. "You'll be auditing in no time."

"I guess that's what it's all about, right?" I still had a headache from all the shouting. I would've asked for an aspirin, but I remembered reading a list of rules on the wall that said that any medication, including aspirin, was strictly forbidden while on the course.

After lunch, I went next door. *Curiouser and curiouser,* I thought, remembering a line from *Alice in Wonderland.* For a moment, I had the feeling I was on as strange a journey as Alice in the book. There was a surreal quality to the past two days.

I did not suspect, even for a minute, that the seemingly innocuous TRs I was doing, supposedly to train me to become a better auditor, were actually a series of extremely sophisticated hypnotic and control techniques that would eventually lead me into a state of unthinking obedience and robotic response. Drill by drill, I unwittingly surrendered my mind and will to the whims of this bizarre organization, an organization to which I would become increasingly enslaved as days and years passed.

Is it possible that a sophisticated system of mind control, masquerading as religion, does exist in this country outside the control and wisdom of the courts and the laws of the land? Was I being lured into spiritual, physical, emotional, and mental bondage without my knowledge or consent?

I had, with complete innocence and trust, sold myself into a subtle slavery from which I would emerge years later raped of my mind, emotions, soul, finances, and twelve years of my life, yet no laws existed to protect my freedom. Psychological kidnapping isn't illegal.

Is it possible for one's mind to be completely controlled by another?

The answer is yes.

During those sunny days in October, part of me was dying, my mind and soul being sucked out by the greedy vampire called Scientology. I wasn't to exist as myself for another twelve years.

CHAPTER SIX

On a Clear Night You Can See Forever

I heard a familiar knock on the door. "0700. Time to get up."
I opened my eyes and felt a sharp pain in the top of my head. *Oh, no,* I thought, knowing what was coming. Unwillingly, I pulled myself to a sitting position, feeling the familiar nausea that swept through me, as the pain in my head intensified. I had a migraine.

Groggily, I headed for the bathroom, hoping a cool shower would work. I knew from past history that I was in for a rough day.

There had been a dreamlike quality to the past few days. *Saving the world is a tough job,* I thought. I'd been on course for three days. For some reason, I took it for granted that the center would be closed on Sunday. I'd been looking forward to a break from the intense course schedule—8:00 AM until 10:30 PM, with two short breaks and an hour for lunch. Invariably, at 11:00 PM after the class muster where we shared our wins, there would be an all-hands called, usually to assemble a mailing, and that would last until 1:00 AM or later.

When Sunday arrived, I was surprised to hear the usual knock at my door. Sunday to Scientologists, I discovered, was just another day in the week. To make things worse, the previous night had been an unusually long all-hands call to mail out the monthly newsletter.

I stood over the basin, waiting for the world to stop spinning. I wondered what people did in Scientology when they were sick. I had already surmised from some of materials on the course that medicine was frowned upon except as a last resort and only after the superior remedies in Scientology had been applied.

"Antonio." I held my throbbing head in both hands, as I looked down at my friend seated at his desk. "What does a Scientologist do for pain?"

"Why? What's wrong?" He looked up in concern.

"A migraine. I've had them before. I think it's from lack of sleep. Do you think maybe I could be excused from course for one day?"

"Well, to do that you'd have to go through Ethics." He looked at me with narrowed eyes. "It would probably be better to try and stay on course."

"Ethics? Why?" The thought of a return visit to the teenage tyrant in the Ethics office was intimidating.

"Because in Scientology there is a saying, 'Sickness equals PTS,'" he said seriously. "Potential Trouble Source," he added, seeing my confused look. "It means you might be PTS or connected to an SP— Suppressive Person. Usually, people only get sick when they're connected in some way to a Suppressive. It's the job of Ethics to help you spot the SP. That and some Dianetics auditing should handle it.

"I'll tell you what," he added, seeing my discouraged expression. "Let me talk with the Course Supervisor, and I'll see if I can give you an assist. Wait here."

He returned a few minutes later. "Come with me." Leading me to one of the offices in the back, he closed the door. "We'll do a touch assist and see if that helps." He pulled the chair into the center of the room and indicated for me to sit.

"OK. I'm just going to give you a command, and I want you to acknowledge me each time I repeat the command. Ready?"

"Sure," I answered, not knowing what to expect.

"All right. Here we go." He pressed his finger to my forehead. "Feel my finger?" he asked gently.

"Yeah."

He pressed his finger against my right temple. "Feel my finger?"

"Uh-huh."

Then I felt his finger on my cheek.

"Feel my finger?"

"Yes."

He continued, exerting pressure with his finger at various locations on my body. There seemed to be a pattern to the way he was working. With each pressure, he asked the same question.

It continued for at least half an hour. I wondered what the effect of this was supposed to be. I found myself becoming curiously relaxed, feeling little shivers of energy up and down my spine like one would feel with a good back rub.

As he continued, I became increasingly drowsy. I actually dozed off into much-needed sleep. As I jerked back awake to keep from falling, Antonio continued the curious process.

I felt my muscles relaxing in response to the contact from his finger. Energy flowed throughout my whole body. After what must have been at least an hour, he stopped suddenly and drew back.

"Well, how do you feel?" he asked.

"I don't believe it. I feel great. The headache is gone. I can't believe you got rid of my migraine. Usually, they last at least two days." I was genuinely surprised. I still felt shivers all over my body.

"That's good," Antonio said modestly. "I'm glad it helped. It probably saved you an unnecessary trip to Ethics." He looked at me and chuckled. "Now you need to go back on course while I write this up as a session."

"Thanks," I said gratefully, as I opened the door.

I retrieved my study pack and took my usual seat. As I resumed my studies, I realized that the nausea and grogginess were gone. I even felt rested. It was strange and amazing.

I opened my pack.

> Auditors have since the first session of
> Scientology been the only individuals

> on this planet in this universe capable of freeing Man.
>
> At times, some will forget or choose to ignore the fact that the auditor is not just another fellow or a guy who works in Scientology. An auditor is a highly trained specialist, no matter what level of auditor. He or she is the only one who can give Man the truth. An auditor is very important in clearing up the planet and this universe. All auditors are appreciated.

I knew that Antonio was a Class-8 auditor, meaning that he had done the highest training level in Scientology. At that time, being a Class 8 was similar to having a PhD in any other subject.

After my experience that morning, I was more ready to believe that what Hubbard said in this policy was true. I smiled to myself. It was reassuring to know that Antonio was my friend. From the beginning, he took a fatherly interest in me. We shared a common interest in the piano. Antonio, I soon discovered, was a brilliant concert pianist.

I continued reading.

> Scientology is a science of life. It is the first entirely Western effort to understand life. All earlier efforts came from Asia or Eastern Europe, and they failed. None of them gave greater security. None of them could change human behavior for the better. None of them, and they bragged about it, could change human intelligence. Scientology is something new under the sun, but young as it is, it is still the only completely and thoroughly tested and validated science of existence.

> Scientology can and does change human behavior for the better. Scientology can and does increase human intelligence, and Scientology can do other things. It is a science of life, and it works. It adequately handles the basic rules of life, and it brings order into chaos.

On another page, I kept reading.

> In all the broad universe there is no other hope for Man than ourselves. Let us face the reality of this thing. The world confronts several crises. Man's inhumanity to man is gaining momentum daily. The time to bring a chaos under control is before it is well begun. We're slightly late as it is. Brutally, there is no other organization on Earth that can slow these down. Factually, there is no other know-how on Earth that can plumb the problems of Man, so if we don't want all of us to be sitting among the charred embers, we had better get busy.
>
> This is no alarmist statement. We are the people who can confront it. Past civilizations have vanished, you see. The Chaldean, Babylonian, Egyptian, Chinese, Hindu, Greek, Roman, and European vanished. Those little beaten-down peasants you see in France were once the proud Romans. Those small, brown men who sell their sisters on the streets of Cairo were once the mighty Egyptians. When those societies looked richest, they had

already started down, like this one.

They all failed, because they had no know-how about Man. Wisdom, real wisdom, could have salvaged any one of them. Wisdom can salvage this one. Scientology can smooth the way, but Scientology hasn't a chance unless we get groups going. You...can do this.

I felt a tap on my shoulder. It was another girl on the course, named Ellie.

"I need someone to do TR 0." She looked at me hopefully. "Do you have time to do it?"

"Sure. It's not like I'm going anywhere."

We spent the rest of the morning staring blissfully into each other's eyes. I experienced the same sensations as I had the first time I did TR 0 with George. When the Supervisor called lunch break, I again felt the expansive serenity and blissed-out timelessness I had before. By the looks of it, so did Ellie.

"That's it! Lunch break!"

I reluctantly came back to earth and shook myself back into normal consciousness. As I walked back to the house for lunch, I noticed that the colors again looked unusually bright. I felt soaring hopefulness inside.

"Oh, Aileen," I said, as I took my place at the table. "I'm so happy to be in Scientology. I just want everyone to know about it. Do you know what I mean?"

"Yes, Dear." Aileen gazed at me fondly. "I've been meaning to talk to you. Antonio and I have been talking, and we'd like you to consider joining us in the Sea Org. That's the most effective way to make a difference in this world. We'll talk about it later." She and Antonio traded glances.

The Sea Org! I thought excitedly. I'd heard many stories in the past few days about the adventures of the most elite group in Scientology. I noticed a poster on the wall at the center. It was a picture of a large ship with many smiling faces waving from the deck and the words, *Be the elite of planet Earth, the cream of the cream. Join the Sea Org.*

Why not? I wondered, serving myself vegetables. *What do I have to lose?* It would be an adventure.

I was still lost in fantasy when the Supervisor called, "That's it!" to begin the afternoon session. I returned to my study pack, determined to keep my mind on what I was reading.

> We are the only people and the only organization on Earth who have the technology and the ambition to attempt a clarification of situations which, in other hands, are considered entirely out of our control, to whit, the atomic bomb and the decay and confusion of societies.
>
> Scientology is today around the world, represented on every continent on Earth. As you read this, this very book is being translated into many non-English tongues and is being distributed to nations whose thronging multimillions have never before been touched by Anglo-American thought.
>
> The use or neglect of this material may well determine the use or neglect of the atomic bomb by Man. Scientology is already winning in this field. In the same period in history, two of the most sweeping forces Man has known have come to fruition: a knowledge of himself and others with Scientology and the

means of destroying himself and all others by atomic fission. Which force wins depends in a large measure on your use of Scientology.

There is not much Earth time. We must work.

The mission of Scientology is not conquest. It is civilization. It is a war upon the stupidity which leads us toward the Last War of All.

With Scientology, man can prevent insanity, criminality, and war. It is for Man to use. It is for the betterment of Man. The primary race of Earth is not between one nation and another today. The only race that matters at this moment is the one being run between Scientology and the atomic bomb. The history of man, as has been said by well-known authorities, may well depend upon which one wins.

I turned another page and continued to read.

Where Earth pursues her gentle way in her orbit about the sun today there will be a black orb seared, scorched, and defaced with ruin, its air polluted with radiation, its surface gouged by pocks, the skeletons of its cities standing black and ruined against a sun which was allowed to set upon the Anglo-American civilization. Perhaps there are other planets, perhaps there will be other times, but here we are right now, and our urgings and our strivings ought to carry forward the civilization which we have about us. Perhaps it would be better to start all over and make another one. I do not happen to think so. I think we can and will continue to create this civilization and continue to bring Man through despite his folly. We know how, and we can do it. It is up to us. It is up to you, and only then, we can say with honesty that it is up to Man.

Later, if we make it, what will be your answer to this question: "Did you help?"

I sat there for a few minutes, lost in thought about my life at the University. What was I doing? Where was I going? Was there any purpose to my life?

The answer was no. Here was something important that I could do to make a difference in the world. What was my dream before? Becoming a music teacher? Here I could help save the world from a possible nuclear disaster. Which was more important?

The answer was already in my mind. It was not a choice. Music could wait. The decision was made. I would join the Sea Org!

I couldn't wait for the break, so I could tell Antonio and Aileen. I knew they'd be happy. For me, it would almost be like having a family. Antonio and Aileen were already closer to me than my real parents had been. They were my spiritual parents. I felt happy and secure. Joining the Sea Org would be like joining a family. Signing the papers would just be a formality. The reality was that, in my soul, I was already a part of the family. I belonged.

"That's it! Break! Fifteen minutes!"

There was the usual sound of chairs scraping the floor, as everyone went outside.

I approached Antonio with a smile. "Antonio, I've decided. I'm joining the Sea Org!"

"That's wonderful." He was sincere. "Let's go share the good news with Aileen." We walked toward the office in the back.

Aileen looked up, surprised, as we entered.

"Aileen," I said breathlessly, "I'm joining. I want to join the Sea Org. I want to help."

Aileen clapped her hands and came over to hug me. "My dear, that's wonderful," she said warmly. "I guarantee you'll never be sorry. You've made a very good decision. We're delighted to have you. Antonio and I were both hoping that you'd come to this decision, but we didn't think it would be so soon! Congratulations!"

"What do I have to do?" I asked eagerly.

"There are just a few things we have to take care of." Aileen pulled some papers from her desk. "We have to go over this questionnaire just to make sure you don't have any incomplete cycles anywhere out in the world."

She began asking questions. Did I have any debts? Any legal problems? Would anyone in my family oppose my decision?

I thought about my parents. They might not be happy about this latest turn of events, but I knew they'd never try to prevent me from doing something I really wanted to do.

"No," I replied.

She continued asking questions. Did I own any property? Did I have children? Was there anything at all that would interfere with my becoming a full-time Scientology staff person?

"None whatsoever," I said, brimming with eagerness.

"All right. Everything seems to be fine." She signed the questionnaire and pulled out another paper from her desk. "Are you ready to sign your contract?" She smiled at me proudly, as she handed me the official-looking form printed on white bond legal paper.

At the top, printed in gold, was the Sea Org symbol of two olive branches surrounding a star. In very large letters were the words *Flag Service Org, SEA ORGANIZATION, Contract of Employment.*

Beneath that were two seahorses in gold flanking a paragraph.

I, _____,
DO HEREBY AGREE to enter
into employment with the SEA
ORGANIZATION and, being of sound
mind, do fully realize and agree to abide by
its purpose which is to get ETHICS IN on
this PLANET AND UNIVERSE and, fully
and without reservation, subscribe to the
discipline, mores, and conditions of this
group and pledge to abide by them.

THEREFORE, I CONTRACT MYSELF
TO THE SEA ORGANIZATION FOR
THE NEXT BILLION YEARS.

There were lines for signatures. I looked at it again. I wasn't seeing things. Perplexed, I looked up at Antonio and Aileen.

"A billion years?" I asked. "Why a billion years?"

Antonio looked across at Aileen. "That's because Ron thinks it will take at least that long to clear the entire universe. After this planet is clear, there are hundreds of thousands of other planets to clear as well. He just wants to be sure that your loyalty is certain. If you're not ready to commit to a billion years, then you're probably not ready to join the Sea Org." He looked at me seriously.

"I think what it is also," Aileen interrupted, "is that being a Sea Org member isn't an easy life. There can be some tough times. If you're not with us 100%, if you're not ready to make a life-and-death commitment, then you won't succeed as a Sea Org member. This is a big decision."

I swallowed and thought again about Michigan, school, and my family. I started to laugh. "I've never thought this far into the future before. I'm not used to thinking in terms of a billion years. You don't have any shorter contracts? Like maybe just a few thousand years for a start?"

Neither of them smiled.

"At the regular Orgs," Antonio explained, "like the LA Org, there are shorter contracts. You can sign up for either two-and-a-half or five years, but in the Sea Org, there's just one contract. This is it."

I sat silently for a moment then slowly picked up the pen on the desk. "Well, here goes." I signed on the blue line. I tried to comprehend a billion years, but my mind got lost after the first few million. "I'm in."

"Splendid." Aileen signed her name on the line below.

Antonio signed as the second witness.

"It's official." Aileen gave a satisfied sigh. "Welcome to the Sea Org, dear. We're glad to have you aboard."

Antonio shook my hand. "Let's all go out to lunch," he suggested, "at a real restaurant to celebrate."

It was hard to think clearly that afternoon, because my mind kept trying to comprehend the enormity of the contract I just signed. One week earlier, I realized with a shock of surprise, I was sitting in class in Ann Arbor worried about my grades. For a minute, I wondered if maybe I had died and progressed to an entirely new life. That couldn't possibly be any stranger than my life.

Aileen gave me a packet of materials to read, to begin the indoctrination process into the Sea Org. I turned to the page at the top and saw the title *YOUR POST.*

> A post in a Scientology organization isn't a job. It's a trust in a crusade.
>
> We are free men and women, probably the last free men and women on Earth. Remember, we'll have to come back to Earth someday no matter what happens to us.
>
> If we don't do a good job now, we may never get another chance. We have an organization. We have a field we must support. We have a chance.

> That's more than we had last time night's
> curtain began to fall on freedom.
>
> So we're using that chance.
>
> An organization such as ours is our best
> chance to get the most done, so we're
> doing it!
>
> L. Ron Hubbard

Just before dinner break, there was a surprise announcement by the Supervisor.

"There will be no class tonight." She gave no explanation. "Class dismissed."

Antonio came up to me, as I was packing my things. "Why don't you come over for dinner? We have a surprise for you tonight."

"And you're not going to tell me what it is, right?" I looked at him mischievously.

"I'm afraid you're just going to have to wait." His eyes were twinkling.

I walked across Alvarado Park with Antonio and Aileen. I was appalled to find that the beautiful park was populated by hundreds of alcoholics. Many were sleeping on benches while others were sprawled on the ground.

Antonio and Aileen shared a small apartment on the other side of the park. As we entered, I was surprised to see a concert-sized grand piano in the living room. "Oh, Antonio," I begged, "play something."

"Just for a few minutes," Antonio said. "We have plans tonight, and we don't want to be late." He sat down and began to play a Scarlatti sonata. I'd never heard Scarlatti played so lightly and effervescently.

"That's wonderful," I enthused when he finished. "It sparkles. Please, play some more."

He began a piece I wasn't familiar with. It sounded like Liszt but it was a piece I hadn't heard before. As Antonio played effortlessly through the complex and brilliant passages, it sounded like a dance.

"That was wonderful." I was enthralled by his playing. "I just want to stay and listen to you play all night. We don't have to go out," I pleaded.

"Oh, yes, we do." Antonio laughed. "By the way, any time you want to come over here in your free time and use the piano, you're welcome to. Julie told us that you're a very accomplished pianist yourself. Next time you come over, when we have more time, we'll listen to you play, too."

"It can wait." I laughed. "There's no way I would play after what I just heard."

We had a pleasant dinner in the tiny kitchen. Antonio was entertaining and told funny stories about recent happenings at the center. After dinner, I helped Aileen with the dishes and asked her about her life before she joined Scientology.

She was from Australia, where she had been a schoolteacher before being introduced to Scientology by a friend. She joined the Sea Org immediately.

"Almost the way you have," she said, looking at me fondly. She spent several years with Ron on the ship, serving as one of his closest assistants.

"What's he really like?" I asked eagerly.

"He's just the most wonderful man you could imagine." She looked at me wistfully. "I hope you have a chance to meet him someday. He's very powerful. When you're near him, you can just feel the power he exudes. And he's so caring. He really cares about all of us. It was his idea to start the Celebrity Center. He believes that artists are special, and that they should have their own center, a protected place where they can create in a safe space."

I was about to ask another question when Antonio interrupted.

"Time to be off," he announced.

We reached Celebrity Center just as it was beginning to get dark. A crowd of people was thronging outside, slowly moving inside. The sign on the door read, *CLEAR NIGHT. ONLY CLEARS AND ABOVE CAN ENTER.*

I looked at Antonio questioningly.

"You're with us," he assured me. "No one will ask any questions. Just act as if you belong."

Aileen had already disappeared into the crowd. Antonio maneuvered over to the far wall where there was more space. There was a ledge against the wall. I quickly climbed up and saw I would have a good view of the stage.

The curtain behind the classroom had been pulled back to reveal the wide stage and a large, open area in which chairs had been set up. Most of the chairs were already filled. A large picture of Hubbard hung on the wall behind the stage.

I looked around the room. Most of the people seemed to be in their twenties or thirties. Many wore unconventional clothing, colorful and "artsy." There was a feeling of subdued excitement in the air. Voices murmured, as people moved to their seats and exchanged greetings with friends.

The air was warm and close in the room. There was a humid sensation from too many bodies. I wiped beads of perspiration from my forehead.

Suddenly, Aileen appeared on the stage and was greeted with riotous applause. Her popularity was obvious. The clapping continued for a long time. Finally, it quieted.

"Welcome to Clear Night," Aileen said. "We have some exciting surprises for you tonight, which I know you'll enjoy. I'm so delighted to see you all and so happy that each one of you could be with us tonight. This will be a very special night.

"The first thing we're going to do tonight is to introduce our new Clears, everyone who has gone Clear since our last Clear Night. Here to introduce them is our special guest, John McMaster!"

Gasps came from the audience. John McMaster was the revered saint of Scientology, the first Clear. His name was well known to everyone in Scientology.

As he entered, a slim figure in a white turtleneck sweater and dark suit, complementing his clear complexion and pearly white hair, the audience stood and began rhythmical applause. Shouts rose. It took several minutes for the applause to die down.

John spoke in a soft and gentle, yet compelling voice. Everyone strained to hear each word. He greeted everyone and began to speak about the ship where Ron was, where he had just been. "Ron sends all his love and his best postulates to all of you. He wants you to know that he's very proud of what you're all doing to expedite the spread of Scientology across the globe. As artists, you each have a vital function in this work, and as artists, you have many unique opportunities to share this wonderful knowledge with those in the world who are ready to receive it. Ron wants you to know that he appreciates what each and every one of you is doing to make this world a better place for everyone, and a space in which all men, including artists, can be free to live and to create. He wanted me to tell you that he loves you all."

As he paused, a cheer went up, then came more applause.

McMaster continued with stories about life aboard the ship and with recent wins Scientology was having all over the world. "It's only a matter of time until we'll achieve a Clear planet, on which to create our New Civilization. Then the aims that Hubbard laid out at the beginning of this great journey will be achieved for all mankind—a world free of illness, insanity, and war, a brave New Civilization where man is free to achieve his dreams. A world which we can probably pass on to our children, knowing that the nightmares of the past will be dreamed no more."

He paused again for applause.

"Now, what you have all been waiting for. We have a list of all those who have become Clear in the past month. Aileen and I will read them off one by one, and they can come forward to receive their certificates. Here we go."

Aileen came up to the mike. "The first Clear is," she paused for effect, "Michael Ryan."

A young man in the front row bounded up on stage. Aileen handed him his certificate and hugged him, then she gave him the microphone.

"Wow, you guys," he began, "I'm telling you, you have all got to do this. This is the most far-out experience you can imagine. I knew it would be good, but it's even more than I ever imagined. I'm so keyed-out. I feel like I'm sitting on top of this planet. I know that nothing is going to get me at effect ever again." He turned to the picture of Ron Hubbard. "Thanks, Ron, for this incredible gift."

He returned the microphone to Aileen and bounded back into the audience. People greeted him with cheers and more rhythmic applause.

John McMaster read off the name of the next new Clear. "Nancy Stephenson."

A young woman walked gracefully up to receive her certificate. Taking the microphone, she looked shyly at the audience.

"I've been in Scientology for almost a decade," she said softly in a European accent. "It has been my privilege to work with Ron at Saint Hill and also on the ship. I knew when I found Scientology that I'd found my new family. I see miracles through the tech like you all have. I can't really express how it feels to be Clear. I guess if you were to imagine the best that you ever felt in your life, then you would have to imagine something ten times better, and you'd have an idea of Clear. Now that I'm Clear I just want to work to bring this miraculous tech to the rest of the planet."

There was more applause.

Several more Clear completions went to the stage to receive their certificates. The speeches became increasingly more fantastic.

One man, who looked to be in his thirties, told of the experiences he was having with exteriorization. "You won't believe this," he told the spellbound audience, "but after I put the body to bed at night, I let the body go to sleep, then I slip out and go anywhere on the planet I want. Last night, I dived through the waves in the

Bahamas. I went over to London and amused myself for a while. Then I took off into space and traveled to several planets far from Earth. You won't believe it until you do this for yourself. All I can tell you is that the tech is there. Ron has laid it all out for us. All we have to do is walk the road he has given us. This really is the Road To Total Freedom."

He retired to the sound of wild applause.

There were more incredible stories. One man spoke of leaving his body at night and preventing a murder in a nearby room. He was able to telepathically disarm the killer and frighten him from the scene.

Another person told about moving clouds and making changes in the weather over the city.

Another Clear reported that he was able to bring about a triple expansion in his business by using the power of his "postulates."

At the end of the speeches, Aileen came to the stage. She turned to a large portrait of Hubbard on the curtain, serving as a backdrop to the stage. "Let's give honor to the man who has made this all possible, L. Ron Hubbard."

Instantly, everyone in the audience stood.

"Hip, hip, hooray!" they shouted, raising their right arms into the air on the last syllable.

"Hip, hip, hooray!" They saluted the larger-than-life-size picture of Ron.

"Hip, hip, hooray!" they shouted a third time, then broke into wild applause.

I looked at Antonio. "Is this for real?"

"Yes." He smiled. "It's for real."

Aileen signaled for quiet. "Now," she said, smiling serenely at the audience, "we're going to have some group processing. After that, a special surprise. Antonio's going to entertain us with some special music."

The crowd quieted.

"We'll begin with some Havingness processing."

I turn to Antonio, about to ask a question, but he motioned me to silence.

"Spot a spot in the room," Aileen said.

Spot a spot? I wondered. *Just spot a spot? How do you do that?"*

Everyone in the audience was silent.

I guess, I thought, *you just pick a place in the space in the room and concentrate on it.* I tried it, but nothing happened.

"Now," Aileen said, "spot another spot in the room."

There was more silence.

"Now spot a spot on the floor."

Heads looked down at the floor.

"Spot a spot on the front wall."

She continued giving commands. The audience silently obeyed.

"Now, without turning around, spot a spot on the back wall. Now, spot a spot in your body. Spot another spot in your body. Spot another spot in the room."

That continued for several minutes. There was no sound from the audience.

"Now are going to take a tour of the universe. Here are your commands. First, be near the Earth."

As before, the audience silently followed her commands.

"OK, now be near the moon. Be near the sun. Be near the moon. Now find a rock. Be inside it. Be outside it. Be in the center of the Earth. Be near Mars. Be at the center of Mars. Be on the surface of Mars."

She gave similar commands using the other planets. Her voice had a hypnotic effect on the audience. "Close your eyes and locate the upper corner of the room behind you."

There was silence.

"Now locate the other upper corner behind you. Hold onto those two corners, and don't think. Now find the third corner behind you. Now find the fourth back corner. Now hold onto all eight corners of the room. Sit back and don't think."

There was a long period of silence. I tried to follow the commands, concentrating mentally on the corners of the room. I wanted to ask someone some questions about what we were doing, but I knew it wasn't the time.

"Now," Aileen's voice sounded brighter, "find someone near you and tell them something about themselves that you like."

The room became noisy, as everyone followed the command.

I looked at Antonio. "I really like your piano playing."

"I like your enthusiasm." He smiled back at me.

"Now find someone else in the room and tell them something that you like about them."

There was more noise, as the audience complied.

"Stay here," Antonio told me. "I have to go up front." He disappeared into the crowd.

The air in the room was stifling. I was glad I wasn't claustrophobic. The humidity was intense, and the temperature was rising from the closeness of so many bodies packed into the room.

Aileen ended the group processing and called Antonio onto the stage. He was greeted with enthusiastic applause.

He sat at the piano and played a few Scarlatti pieces, obviously a specialty of his. Then he played Chopin—some preludes and a mazurka.

Then he stopped, waiting for silence from the audience. When they were quiet, he smiled and said, "Space music." He looked at me and winked.

Then he began improvising. I sat back to enjoy the music. It was unlike any music I ever heard, almost pure sound. It was easy to let my mind wander and visualize scenes in distant space, mysterious planets, the milky haze of the galaxies, shooting stars hurtling through space. I listen admiringly to the impressionistic sounds he got from the piano, wondering how he was able to create such effects. Far too soon, the music ended.

The audience jumped to their feet, calling Antonio back for several curtain calls.

Aileen came back on stage with Antonio, and again she turned to the picture of Ron on the back wall. The audience began clapping rhythmically.

"Hip, hip, hooray!" they shouted with wild applause.

"Hip, hip, hooray!"

"Hip, hip, hooray!"

The applause continued for a long, long time. I glanced at my watch and saw it was nearly midnight. Antonio reappeared at my side.

"Well," he teased, "how'd you like it?"

"Antonio, this was really great. I loved your playing, especially the space music. I wanted to listen to you all night."

People began to filter out the narrow doorway. I said good-bye to Antonio and walked back to the house. Whatever the priorities had been in my life just hours before were replaced with a single, driving ambition against which all other goals dwarfed in importance.

I looked up at the stars and the bright western sky. Only one thing was important—I wanted to be a Clear!

CHAPTER SEVEN

The Date of the Incident Is 520 BC

"Miss Wakefield." Startled, I looked up from the policy letter I'd been engrossed in, to find the Course Supervisor standing beside me with a slender young woman with thick red hair.

"This is Kim. She's looking for a PC (preclear). I've looked in your folder, and you're eligible for Dianetics auditing."

"Great!" I was anxious to start on the road to Clear. Part of being a student on the Dianetics course meant that, in addition to auditing others, the student would also receive auditing from another student. Three successful sessions were required to complete the course. This was my chance.

We walked to Kim's small apartment several blocks away, exchanging small talk.

"Have a seat," Kim offered, sitting and adjusting the E-meter in preparation for the session. "Pick up the cans, please." She continued adjusting the meter. "First we'll check your rudiments."

I looked at her blankly.

"Here." She handed me the Scientology dictionary.

> A rudiment is that which is used to get the PC in shape to be audited. Rudiments consist of ARC breaks, PTPs, or W/Hs.

I groaned. "Why is it, that when I read these definitions, I end up even more confused?"

"Which word don't you understand?" she asked patiently.

"ARC breaks." I looked it up in the dictionary before she could speak.

> ARC. A word from the initial letters of
> Affinity, Reality, and Communication,
> which together equate to Understanding. It
> is pronounced by stating its letters, A-R-C.

"Now look up ARC break," Kim suggested.
I looked on the next page.

> ARC break. A sudden drop or cutting of
> one's affinity, reality, or communication
> with someone or something.

"I had the idea," I thought out loud, "from listening to people talk around the center, that an ARC break meant you were upset with someone."

"Exactly. If you're in ARC with someone, then you have high affinity with them. In other words, you like them a lot. You have high reality with them in that you both have a high level of agreement about most things. You're able to communicate well, because of your shared affinity and reality.

"Think of ARC as a triangle with three points for affinity, reality, and communication. All three together add up to understanding. If any point of the triangle becomes affected, it will, in turn, affect the other two points."

I began to understand. "So if you disagree with someone about something, which would be a lowering of the reality part of the triangle, then there would be less affinity between you, and it would be more difficult to communicate."

"Exactly. As a result, there would be less overall understanding between you. That's how it works."

"If you decided to stop talking to someone, then you would have less affinity for them, and there would be less shared reality between you. If you had less affinity for someone, say maybe they moved away to a different town, then there would be less communication between you, and there would be less shared reality. OK. I think I've got it." I felt triumphant.

"Are there any other words in the definition you didn't understand?"

"Yes." I looked up the definition again. "PTP." I looked it up in the dictionary.

> Present Time Problem. A special problem that exists in the physical universe now, on which the PC has his attention fixed.

I looked at Kim. "So it's just a problem, right? Something going on in my life right now?"

"That's right. That's all there is to it. Now what about W/Hs?" She pronounced it "withholds."

"I was afraid you were going to ask me that." I laughed and turned to the W's.

> Withhold. A withhold is something that the PC did that he isn't talking about; an unspoken, unannounced transgression against a moral code.

"In other words," I paraphrase, "something bad that I did that I haven't told anyone about. That's easy enough. Now can we audit?"

"Sure. Let me just clear your rudiments." Kim picked up her pen and began writing on the paper next to her E-meter. "Do you have an ARC break?" She looked at me intensely with what I recognized as TR 0.

"If that means being upset with anyone, no. I'm not upset with anyone. Everyone has been very nice." I smiled.

"That's clean." She checked her meter. "Do you have a present-time problem?" She studied the meter. "That reads.... Is there a problem in your life right now?"

"Yes. I guess it's the fact that I don't have any money. There are some things I need to buy, but I spent all my money on the course.

I guess I could call my dad and ask him to send me a small spending allowance. That would solve the problem." I looked at Kim.

"That's clean. Now, do you have any withholds? I get a big read on that. Can you tell me about it?"

"Yeah. I know exactly what it is. I haven't told my parents about my joining the Sea Org. I don't know how to explain it to them. How do you tell your parents that you just signed up for a billion years in someone's private navy?" I laughed, then I thought for a moment.

"Maybe I could tell them that I'm working out here for Celebrity Center and not mention the billion years right away. They wouldn't understand it, anyway." I was suddenly aware of how much my thinking had changed in one week. Things that were important a week earlier were much different from the things that were important now.

I sighed. "How do you explain something like Scientology to your parents? Or for that matter, to anyone who doesn't know anything about it? It's not exactly easy to explain."

"OK." She kept her TRs in. I knew, according to the TRs, she wasn't allowed to do anything other than just acknowledge what I originated.

"I'd like to indicate that you had charge on 'telling your parents about joining the Sea Org.'" She looked down at the meter. "Your needle is floating. We can now begin Dianetics."

"I'm ready!" I looked at her brightly.

"OK. According to your last session, which was a touch assist you had with Antonio, you complained of a migraine headache. Are there any feelings connected with that?"

I knew by then that in Dianetics, one could only run actual feelings. "Migraine headache" was too broad a concept to run as a Dianetics item.

"Yes. The feeling is a pain in the top front of my head."

"OK. Yes, you got a big read on that. We will run the item 'a pain in the top front of my head.' Now, locate an incident containing 'a pain in the top front of my head.'"

"Yesterday."

"All right. How long did it last?"

"Just a couple of hours. It went away while Antonio was doing the touch assist."

"OK. Move to the beginning of the incident and tell me when you are there."

"I'm there."

"Thank you. What do you see?"

"I see me waking up in the morning with this pain in my head." I closed my eyes to concentrate on the memory.

"All right. Scan through to the end of the incident and tell me what happened."

"I got up, showered, and went to the center to find Antonio. He gave me a touch assist, and the headache went away." As I spoke, the image grew more and more vivid in my mind.

"Is the incident erasing or going more solid?"

"It's definitely more solid."

"All right. Locate an earlier incident containing a pain in the top front of your head."

Another picture came to mind. With my eyes closed, I said, "OK. This happened a long time ago."

"When was it?" Kim asked softly.

"It was when I was about four." It was strange that I could visualize the images clearly as if it happened the previous day.

"OK. How long did it last?"

"A few hours. I had to have some stitches in my forehead."

"Move to the beginning of the incident and tell me when you are there."

"OK. I'm there." The picture became more vivid.

"Scan through to the end of the incident and tell me what happened," she commanded gently.

"Well, I was four, and I was playing with my brother when he hit me in the head with a toy shovel. He hit me really hard. I needed several stitches in my forehead." I studied the colorful image in my mind.

"Is the incident erasing or going more solid?"

"I guess it's more solid. I can see it quite vividly." I kept my eyes closed.

"All right. Locate an earlier incident containing a pain in the top front of your head."

I looked into the darkness. "There's nothing there."

"OK. Just keep looking. Tell me if anything comes to your mind."

I peered into the darkness. "I just don't see anything at all."

"All right. Let's go back to the incident with your brother. Is that incident erasing or going more solid?"

"I can still see that one quite clearly."

"OK. See if anything comes to your mind."

"I just see blackness. I can't see anything. Nothing is coming to mind." I opened my eyes and blinked at her.

"All right." She smiled at me. "We'll take a break, so I can get some instructions from the C/S."

"Did I do something wrong?" I had the feeling things hadn't gone the way they should.

"No." She started packing her things. "Sometimes, people have trouble, at first, seeing their past lives. You might have to go for a Review."

"Review?"

"Yes. There are some special remedies for people who have trouble seeing their past lives. It doesn't take long, and then I can take you back into session."

We walked back to the center, not talking much on the way. I had the nagging feeling that I failed and Kim was disappointed in me, although she didn't say anything to lead me to that belief.

Back on course, I open my study packs where I left off. I was just beginning the last section of the course which was called Dianetics Theory. There was a short book to read called *Dianetics, Evolution of a Science*, by Hubbard. In it, he defined some of the basic Dianetics concepts.

He wrote that the analytical mind functioned like a computer. It had color-visio, tone audio, odor, tactile, and organic memory recall. *It should be able to recall any perception, even the trivial, asleep and awake from the beginning of life to death.*

The mind, he explained, was composed of memory banks filed by time. Those banks *contain a complete color-visio record of a person's whole life. Every perception observed in a lifetime is to be found in the banks.*

According to Hubbard, the reason we couldn't remember everything was the existence of the reactive mind, the record of all painful experiences from a lifetime. Each picture in the reactive mind had as its content pain and/or unconsciousness. It was that mind that kept the analytical mind from functioning at an optimal level. Through auditing, he said, the reactive mind could be erased.

In Dianetics, the memories and the reactive mind were called *engrams*. They could be restimulated later in life by events with similar content.

For example, if two-year-old Mary was knocked over and bitten on the arm by a black dog, seeing a black dog thirty years later might restimulate a mysterious pain in the arm.

According to Dianetics theory, when a person, through auditing, made the connection between the pain in the arm in the earlier memory and was able to relive the earlier memory, the pain would vanish. According to Hubbard, 90% of all illness was psychosomatic in nature, and all would submit to the Dianetics technique.

At the end of the book, I found a familiar-sounding passage.

> Man's efforts to free man by enslaving
> him in social and personal aberrations was
> the wrong equation, the road to nowhere.
> In ages past, the hold of the slavery of
> aberration has been broken by the opening
> up of new lands and the appearance of new
> races.

> But now we've got a science to break it
> and a technology to be applied.
>
> Up there are the stars. Down in the arsenal
> is an atom bomb.
>
> Which one is it going to be?

I began reading the book *Dianetics: Modern Science of Mental Health,* by Hubbard. On the inside flap of the book jacket, I read:

> Dianetic therapy is a new science which works with the invariability of physical science in the field of the human mind. Dianetics will help the reader to eliminate any psychosomatic illness. Dianetics will help the reader to achieve up to one-third more efficiency than present capacity. Dianetics is the most advanced and the most clearly presented method of psychotherapy and self-improvement ever discovered.
>
> Psychosomatic ills such as arthritis, migraine, ulcers, allergies, asthma, coronary difficulties (psychosomatic about one-third of all heart trouble cases), tendonitis, bursitis, hysterical paralysis, and eye trouble have all responded, as intended by the therapist, without failure in any case.

In the introduction to the book, the promises continued:

> The creation of Dianetics is a milestone for Man comparable to his discovery of fire and superior to his inventions of the wheel and the arch.

> Dianetics, (from the Greek *dianoua*, (meaning thought), is the science of the mind. Far simpler than physics or chemistry, it compares with them in the exactness of its axioms and is on a considerably higher echelon of usefulness. The hidden source of all psychosomatic ills and human aberration has been discovered, and skills have been developed for their invariable cure.
>
> Dianetics is an adventure. It is an exploration into *terra incognita*, the human mind, that vast and hitherto unknown region half an inch back of our foreheads.
>
> The discoveries and developments, which made the formulation of Dianetics possible, occupied many years of exact research and careful testing. The trail is blazed, the routes are sufficiently mapped for you to voyage in safety into your own mind and recover there your full inherent potential, which is not, we now know, low but very, very high.
>
> You are beginning an adventure. Treat it as an adventure, and may you never be the same again.

The goal of Dianetics is the Clear, described in the book as follows:

> A Clear can be tested for any and all psychoses, neuroses, compulsions, and repressions (all aberrations) and can be examined for any autogenic

> (self-generated) diseases referred to as psychosomatic ills. These tests confirm the Clear to be entirely without such ills or aberrations. Additional tests of his intelligence indicate it to be high above the current norm. Observation of his activity demonstrates that he pursues existence with vigor and satisfaction.

The only Clears I knew were Antonio and Aileen, and they certainly seemed to have no problems. At lunch, I told Antonio about my session.

"Antonio, I'm confused about past lives. Are there some people in Scientology who just can't remember their past lives?" I asked.

"Well, sooner or later, it's my experience that everyone will remember their past lives," Antonio said. "For some people, it just takes more time."

When we returned to the center, he handed me a book. "Maybe this will help," he said kindly.

I took the book back to my seat. The cover read, *Have You Lived before This Life?* I opened to the introduction.

> In the past, the term reincarnation has mystified Man. The definition has been corrupted. The word has been taken to mean to be born again in different life forms, whereas its actual definition is to be born again into the flesh or into another body. In order that there can be rebirth, something must enter in. This is the being, the person himself. It is YOU.
>
> The existence of past lives is proven in Scientology.

An adventure awaits you. It is a journey through restored consciousness of ages past. Once regained, your own natural memory of past experiences can never be blotted from your recollection again. Your journey is completely uninhibited by synthetic experiences, drugs, or hypnosis of any form, for it is the process of awakening of awareness, of restored knowledge and clarity of being.

With Scientology, you are the judge of your own certainty in your past experiences, because you will know for yourself without reservation what they are. After all, you were there!

The concept of reincarnation and Man's belief in the past and future continuum is as old as Man himself. It can be traced to the beginnings of thirty-one primitive cultures and has dominated almost every religion through history as a pivotal belief.

The Egyptians, Hindus, Buddhists, Jainists, Sikhists, Brahmans, NeoPlatonists, Christians, Romans, Jews, and Gnostics all believed in reincarnation and the rebirth cycle.

It was a fundamental belief in the Roman Catholic Church until 553 AD, when a company of four monks held the Synod of Constantinople, (without the Pope present) and decided the belief could not exist. They condemned the teachings of reincarnation as heresy, and it was at this

> time that references to it were expunged from the Bible.
>
> Without reference to the subject as the written word, the belief fell to the mystics and spiritualists of the Middle Ages. These, too, were defeated, but the belief persisted and again was rediscovered in the 19th century in the beginnings of psychology.
>
> Freud and Jung acknowledged Man's belief in his own immortality and reincarnation. Their mistake was only in assigning this basic truth to imagination or fantasy.
>
> Today, in Scientology, the stigma of the subject has been erased, and verification of the existence of past lives is a fact.
>
> Through reading this book, it is hoped that you will rediscover for yourself the verity of your own existence, no matter how long ago forgotten.
>
> To some, these facts may come as a surprise. To others, it may be as casual as looking at an old photo album. But to everyone it will be a unique and enlightening adventure into the past, all in the course of discovering a brighter future.

The book consisted of forty-two case histories, all of which had been resolved by the remembering of past lives. I read through some of them.

In one account of a man who complained of chronic fatigue, the problem was resolved when the person remembered having been a coolie in 19th-century China.

Another case history reported:

This takes place nine galaxy periods
ago. I was a male, born of space parents.
At the age of five, I was already on the
lookout for brothels. At nine years of age,
I asked my father if I could join the space
academy. However, this does not occur
until I am fourteen. When I am sixteen,
I kill my father while fighting on the
planet, and I join a spaceship. I learn all
about spaceship drills, take-offs, et cetera.
There is homosexuality, as only officers are
allowed women.

In another case, the engram "started on a
planet of perfection 1,600 years ago. By
that, I mean everything was orderly and
routine. My part on this planet was a sort of
engineer in a big powerhouse that supplied
the energy by means of beams to feed the
machines that were in use for the welfare
of the people." The person was eventually
killed with a space pistol.

In yet another history, "The incident was
located on the E-meter and has happened
3,225 years ago. I was positioned in North
Africa near the coast. I was the leader
of that sector of the Roman army. There
were only five such sectors in existence,
reaching around the coast to Europe."
The person later died a mysterious death
by inhaling a powder emitted by a white
circular object in a cave.

In another report the person said that the
incident was "55,000,000,000,000,000,

000 years ago. I was in the sea and had thoughts only for manta rays...."

Another history took place in Italian Somaliland in South Africa in the 17th or 18th century. Another one was in Tibet in 1500 AD. Another took place in 11th century Norway. Another was a monk in England in 1703. Another one experienced a death 2 billion years ago when he landed by mistake on a planet which had been taken over by "black magic operators."

When break was called, I went out and sat by myself at the end of the community log. Kris came over to me.

"You're awfully quiet today. What's up?" She sat beside me.

"It's all this past-life stuff." I shook my head. "I just can't seem to see them. I had a session this morning. When the auditor told me to find an earlier incident, all I could see was darkness. I don't know why. I'm not sure whether to believe in this stuff or not." I looked at her with a troubled expression.

"Well, I had trouble at first," she admitted. "After a while, I just started seeing them. Once you get used to it, it isn't hard at all. It isn't anything to worry about. I just had the attitude that, well, if I saw anything, fine. If I didn't, fine. The only way to know for sure whether they exist for you is just wait and see what happens. No one else can tell you what to believe. Ron says,

'What's true for you is true for you.' Just because something is true for me doesn't mean it will be true for you."

"Thanks, I guess." I stared thoughtfully at the sky. "If they're really there, then I want to see them. If I really did live before, then I want to know who I was."

"Don't worry. It'll come. I think almost everyone here had the same problem at first. You get over it."

I heard my name called from inside the center.

"You're to have a review session," the Supervisor said, as I approached her desk. "Down the hall, second room to your right."

I followed her directions to an open door. A man in his twenties sat with his back to me at a table with an E-meter in the middle of it. I knocked, and he looked around.

"Hi," he welcomed me. "I'm Brad. I'm going to give you a review session. Close the door, please." He indicated I should sit in the opposite chair. "You can pick up the cans. We're just going to start where your auditor left off this morning. First, we'll fly your ruds." Seeing that I didn't understand, he laughed. "I'm sorry. That just means I'm going to check your rudiments like your auditor did this morning. ARC break, present-time problems, withholds. Remember?"

"Oh, yeah. I remember. I think everything is OK."

"Well, we'll just check. Do you have an ARC break? You had a read on that. Any idea what it might be?" He looked at me with the now familiar TR 0.

"Well, maybe. It's just that I'm upset that I can't remember my past lives. I've been reading about it all day. Maybe, I'm not like everyone else. Maybe, I just can't remember." I felt discouraged.

"That's all right. We'll just see what happens. There's nothing to worry about." He seemed unconcerned.

"OK," he continued. "The feeling you were running was 'a pain in the top front of your head,' right? You remembered an incident when you were four and had stitches in your forehead. Do you remember that incident?"

"Oh, sure." I closed my eyes. "I can see it clearly."

"Is it erasing or becoming more solid?"

"It's very clear. I guess it's getting more solid." I concentrated on the mental image.

"That's good." Brad was reassuring. "Now locate an earlier incident containing a pain in the top front of your head. Just take your time and tell me about anything that comes to your mind. Anything at all. Even if it seems silly. Just take your time."

I felt almost hypnotized by his calm, soothing voice.

"That's it. Even if it's just a word that comes to your mind, let me know when you see or think of anything."

"All I see is blackness," I said slowly. "It's black, kind of reddish black. And my head is hurting."

"All right," Brad continued gently. "When was it?"

"I feel like it might be when I was being born."

"Good. How long did it last?"

"I don't know. Maybe a couple of hours."

"OK. Now move to the beginning of the incident and tell me when you're there."

"All right. I guess I'm there," I answered uncertainly.

"OK. What do you see?"

"I just see this reddish blackness, and it seems like I'm inside something. I feel like something is pressing all over me. My head is hurting. It feels as if something is squeezing me. It's like I'm being born."

"Excellent." Brad sounded pleased. "Now move through the incident to a point two hours later and tell me what happened."

I visualized a birth scene. "OK. I just feel this pressure and pain in my head. Then I see this baby being born and held by the doctor. I see it like I'm looking from across the room, but I think it's me who's being born." I stared at the image in my mind.

"All right!" Brad sounded genuinely happy. "Now is the incident erasing or going more solid?"

"More solid, I guess. I can see it pretty clearly." I answered as honestly as I could.

"All right. You're doing fine. Now locate an earlier incident that contains a pain in the top front of your head," he commanded firmly.

Looking again into the darkness, I wondered if it was this hard for everyone. I still didn't see anything. "Nothing. I don't see anything. I'm trying, but I don't see anything at all. Just blackness." I felt like a failure.

"That's OK," Brad encouraged. "Just keep your eyes closed and tell me anything that comes into your mind. Anything at all. An image, or a word, it can be anything. Don't try to force it. Let it come naturally."

I peered into the darkness in my mind. Then I thought of something. "A horse. It's a horse. I see a horse." I looked at the developing image in my mind.

"OK," Brad said cautiously. "Can you see anything else?"

"I just see this horse. I'm galloping across a field."

"Good. That's good. Now when was it?"

"I don't know. I guess sometime in the 18th century." I said the first thing that came to my mind.

"OK. How long did it last?"

"Not long. I think just a few minutes."

"All right. Now move to the beginning of the incident and tell me when you're there."

I tried to follow his command.

"What do you see?" he asked.

"Well, I see myself in this stable. I think it's in England. There's a big stone castle. This man is helping me onto a horse. I think it's my father. I feel like he loves me very much. It seems like he's warning me about something. To be careful. He knows I'm still very inexperienced at riding, and he's telling me to be careful and not to go too fast." The picture developed before my eyes as I spoke.

"All right," Brad said quietly, "now scan through to the end of the incident."

I sat in silence, trying to see the scene before my eyes. "OK." I looked at Brad.

"Tell me what happened."

I closed my eyes again. "I get on this horse, and I'm riding across these fields. I'm feeling really wonderful. I love the feeling of freedom, as I ride through the beautiful countryside. We're coming to a brook. I kick the horse, spurring him on to jump over the brook. I lose control. The horse is galloping really fast, and I lose control of the reins. The next thing I know, I'm falling into the brook, and I hit my head on a rock. I feel cold water across my face, then I lose consciousness. I think I died." I opened my eyes and looked at Brad.

"Do you think that really happened?" I asked him. "It's not just my imagination?"

"I'm not allowed to evaluate for you," he replied matter-of-factly. "That would be a violation of the Auditor's Code. All I can tell you is that what's true for you is true for you. And I'm also not allowed to invalidate you. The test of it will be whether your migraines disappear. There may, however, be other somatics involved in your migraines. You will have to audit them one at a time." He looked across the table at me and smiled. "Is the last picture erasing or going more solid?"

"I think it's erasing." The picture was getting smaller and smaller. I started laughing. "One summer, my parents took me on vacation to a ranch in Texas. We rode horses every day. I was miserable through the whole vacation. Come to think of it, I had a migraine on that trip. Now I understand why!"

"I'd like to indicate that your needle is floating," he informed me with a smile.

"OK. End of session!" he said in a loud voice. "You can put down the cans." He reached for the cans and turned off the meter.

"Let's go find the Examiner," he said, following me from the room.

At the end of the hall was a very small room, a closet actually, with the Examiner sign above the door.

I heard a voice call, "Just a minute!" and looked back to see a young woman running toward me.

"You first." She pointed me into the room. I sat down and picked up the cans.

"Your needle is floating," she informed me with a smile. "That's it."

I set down the cans.

"You can return to class now."

I sat down and thought about the session I just had. I thought about the girl riding in the English countryside. It seemed real enough. Was it possible? I remembered how we used to sit and read Edgar Cayce's books at the coffee house.

I can't wait to tell them about this, I thought. *I can go back and tell them there's a way they can remember their own past lives. They'll love it!*

After my review with Brad, I had no more trouble with past lives.

The following morning, I again followed Kim to her apartment. After we were situated, and she had done the required rudiments check, she looked at me earnestly.

"Are there any other feelings associated with having a migraine?" she asked.

"Yes," I said immediately. "I get this awful feeling of nausea in my stomach."

"That reads." She looked at me triumphantly. "We are going to run 'a feeling of nausea in your stomach.'"

Again we went through the Dianetics procedure, command by command. I was able to recall several times during this lifetime when I had the nausea. Then she asked for an earlier incident.

"I see something. I'm in another city, and I'm in a room underground. I'm a prisoner, and I'm dying."

"When was it?" Kim asked.

"I think it was around 520 BC."

"OK. How long did it last?"

"It lasted for a couple hours." Again, a picture developed before my eyes.

"Move to the beginning of the incident and tell me when you're there."

"OK. I'm there."

"All right. Scan through to the end of the incident."

After a few minutes of quiet, I said, "OK. I'm at the end."

"What happened?"

"I was a prisoner in Greece. They gave me poison to drink. It made me really sick to my stomach. Finally, I died."

"OK. Is the incident erasing or going more solid?"

"More solid."

"OK. Locate an earlier incident containing a feeling of nausea in your stomach."

I looked into the darkness, and the picture came right away. It was getting easier. "I'm in some kind of implant station."

"All right. What is the date of the incident?"

"About 35,000 BC."

"Good. How long did it last?"

"Not long. It happened really fast. A few seconds."

"OK. Move to the beginning of the incident and tell me when you're there."

"I'm there."

"Good. Now scan through to the end of the incident and tell me what happened."

"OK. I'm in this implant station. It's all gray inside. I feel like I'm spinning around and around. While I'm spinning around, I'm being shown pictures. The spinning gets faster and faster, then I'm unconscious. That's all there is. It's an implant."

The picture erased. I opened my eyes and looked at Kim. "I guess that's why I never like carnival rides that go around like that. They made me sick to my stomach."

Kim ended the session, and we headed for the Examiner. After one more successful session, she would graduate from the course. She was happy.

That was how we did Dianetics. That's how people in Scientology are doing Dianetics today. At different times during my career in Scientology, I "relived" a birth in 1896, service in the French resistance during the Second World War, and soldiering in the Roman army in 200 AD. I studied medicine in Egypt, lived as a caveman in the jungle, died of the plague in the Middle Ages, and was a prehistoric animal in 14,027,050. I survived a whole series of interesting implants, lived many lives, and died many deaths on other planets and in other times. I was a villain, a nun, an Indian, an artist, a particle in space, and many other things. In one life, I learned to my amusement, I knew Beethoven. I filed that away to tell Julie when I saw her again.

That was how we did Dianetics.

That's how 40,000 people in this country and approximately 100,000 people in other countries are doing Dianetics today. "May you never be the same again," Hubbard hoped for us all. I probably never will be.

As time passed for me in the sheltered and protective womb of Scientology, and as I had more and more auditing, the reality of the outside world ceased to exist for me, and the only reality I knew or cared about was that contained within Scientology.

The lines between this strange reality and mere fantasy became increasingly blurred over the years, as I was subjected to more and more auditing and more and more Scientology propaganda. I eventually regressed to a state of mind that was, for all practical purposes, psychotic—a psychosis that had its roots in the psychologically destructive, mind-numbing and reality-blurring practice of Dianetic auditing that I received during my very first days in Scientology.

Scientology was, for me, truly the road to nowhere.

CHAPTER EIGHT

Star Trek for Real

Los Angeles, I decided, was a city of contrasts. On my breaks from course, I frequently wandered down to Alvarado Street to buy a twenty-five-cent ice cream from the Jewish delicatessen on the corner of Alvarado and Eighth Streets, or to browse in one of the seedy discount stores on the streets bordering the park. The oppressive squalor of MacArthur Park was a revelation to me. Having been raised in well-scrubbed Midwest suburbs, I was never exposed to the legitimate poverty I saw for the first time.

What irony, I thought each time I walked through the park on my frequent visits to have lunch or dinner with Antonio and Aileen in their small apartment on Lafayette Park Place. The park had a pristine quality with bright, flowering bushes in all shades of red, orange, and yellow blooming unashamedly even in winter. Small ponds were laced with white bridges, and the grass was a deep, healthy shade of green.

The park and the streets around it were the skid row of Los Angeles. Hundreds of alcoholics wandered aimlessly on the streets, begging for the money to satisfy their demonic thirst. Bag ladies, dressed in layers of ragged clothes, passed by, pulling their shopping carts and carrying on monologues with invisible companions. The beauty of the small park was endlessly dotted with the figures of drunks who sprawled on the many benches or lay on the ground sleeping off the effects of the previous night's binge.

Los Angeles, I later discovered, was most beautiful in winter when the smog wasn't as oppressive as in late summer and fall.

I loved the mountain ridges visible on the distant horizon that seemed to provide a protective presence over the city. I saw ragged hills to the west with tiny homes nestled into the cliffs. When there was no smog, the city stretched clearly visible for miles in all directions, a seemingly infinite carpet of human habitation.

For the first few months of my adventure in Scientology, my world consisted only of the center, the park, and the apartment on Lafayette Park Place. Gradually, my universe began to expand. Occasionally, Aileen granted me welcome absences from course to run errands for her to the other nearby Scientology centers. Sometimes, there were envelopes or messages to deliver to the executives at the LA Org, the center on nearby Ninth Street where the Scientology "lower levels" were delivered to noncelebrities.

The curriculum at the Org was similar to that offered at Celebrity Center—the lower levels of Scientology, including Dianetics and Levels 0-4. An auditor trained to deliver these levels was known in Scientology as a "Class-4 auditor."

In the lobby of the Org was a huge picture of Hubbard in his nautical gear, gazing out benevolently at all who entered the room. Sometimes, as I passed through the room, I gazed back in reverence at the portrait, looking into the eyes that seemed to stare right through me. The portrait seemed so lifelike that I often wondered, as I looked up at my guru, if he could read my thoughts or see into my mind as I passed. Did he, like God, know everything about me? I felt a hundred withholds stirring in my subconscious mind, as I passed by the all-seeing visage of Hubbard.

On other errands, I was sent to the smaller, but equally well-kept, building owned by Scientology on the diagonal corner from the LA Org. This was known as the Advanced Org or AO. In that building, the advanced OT levels of Scientology were administered. I was only allowed in the lobby. Only those who were on the secret upper levels were allowed access to the rooms farther inside the building.

In the lobby, the OTs, people on the OT levels, sat silently waiting for their next C/S, instructions for their next auditing session.

Everything in the AO was carried on in hushed tones that seemed to imply the presence of activities of extreme significance in secrecy. The staff at the AO were all uniformed Sea Org members. They saluted each other constantly, walked and talked with great briskness, and seemed filled with the great importance of their mission.

In contrast was the American Saint Hill Organization, ASHO, located several blocks north on Temple Street. In comparison to AO, ASHO seemed somewhat disorganized. It was a much-larger building in which Scientologists polished up their auditing skills on the weighty Saint Hill Special Briefing Course, which Hubbard developed at his mansion in England called Saint Hill. That course consisted of all the materials of levels 0-4, with the addition of hundreds of tape-recorded messages from Hubbard. It was rumored that to pass the Briefing Course, a student must listen to 600 tape-recorded messages of Hubbard, each 60-90 minutes long. Anyone who completed the Briefing Course was known in Scientology as a "Class-6 auditor."

At ASHO, two important courses were given—Power and Solo—which were the last levels before a person could become Clear.

One day, as I was doing an errand for Aileen at ASHO, I sat in the lobby waiting for a message to take back to Aileen and observed a curious event. Just off the lobby to the right was a door. I saw a uniformed Sea Org member walk up to the door carrying a glass of water and small plate of what appeared to be bread crusts. The Sea Org member took a ring of keys from his pocket, unlocked the door, and passed the bread and water to someone on the other side. He relocked the door and walked off.

I looked questioningly at the receptionist who sat across me. "Who was that?"

"Oh, that was the MAA."

I knew that meant the Master at Arms, the Ethics Officer.

"Who's in the closet?"

"It's just someone writing up his O/Ws." Her tone was unconcerned. "He's been in there for three days and nights."

"Why would it take someone three days and nights to write up his overts and withholds? How can someone have done that many things wrong?"

"Because he has to write up his whole track O/Ws," she replied, beginning to be annoyed by my questions. "He has to write up all the overts and withholds he has had in all his lifetimes. Sometimes, that can take days. He can't come out until the MAA is satisfied that he's totally clean. But it's worth it, because when he comes out, you'll see a totally different person."

I'll bet, I thought, stunned by the practice. *What else do they do in the name of Ethics?*

Later, I asked Antonio about the strange disciplinary procedure.

"Yes," he admitted. "Sometimes it's necessary to be really rough on people. But the tech won't work on a person unless his ethics are in. If that's what it takes to get his ethics in, then that's what it takes. It's really doing him a favor. When he comes out of the closet, he'll thank the Ethics Officer for helping him get his ethics in."

I had to be satisfied with that explanation.

Whenever I returned to ASHO on an errand, I always glanced at the closet and wondered if anyone was inside, writing up his O/Ws.

Occasionally, Aileen excused me from class to go next door to help prepare lunch or dinner for the fifty or so people who ate at the house on Burlington Street. Unfortunately, that experience removed my appetite for future meals. One of my tasks was to strain the milk for maggots. Another time, I sifted through heads of lettuce that were filled with worms, trying to salvage enough usable pieces to make a salad.

On another day, Aileen called me into her office and said, "I want you to help at the nursery. They're short-staffed."

I followed her directions and walked twenty or more blocks to a small, windowless building on Franklin Street. *So this is where they keep the children,* I thought, suddenly realizing I'd seen no young children in the weeks I'd been in Scientology, even though I knew many of the staff were married.

As I passed the fenced backyard, I saw a dozen toddlers wandering around in the dirt, clothed only in diapers. There was no grass, just several large trees surrounded by dirt. The children had no toys and played with each other or used their hands to draw pictures in the dirt.

I went to the door on the far side of the building on which was a small blue and white sign that read, *Cadet Org, Church of Scientology.*

I was allowed in, and, as I looked around, I saw a dismal sight. The walls of the rooms and the hall were painted stark white. The floors were dull gray, dirty linoleum. There were no pictures on the walls, no decorations of any kind. Wandering through the halls and the two rooms, I saw several dozen children dressed only in diapers and T-shirts. Most looked as if they hadn't been bathed recently. Several carried bottles, but most wandered in the hall or slept on the bare floor. The rooms were bare of furniture, and there were no toys, books, or any of the normal, familiar signs of childhood. I smelled urine in the room, and many small voices cried plaintively.

A young woman in a Sea Org uniform came up to me and greeted me, introducing herself as Colleen. She was one of two staff members in charge of all the children.

"Where do you keep their toys and books?" I asked.

"They don't have any," she replied expressionlessly. "Children are down statistics, and you don't reward down statistics. That's in the tech."

"But what do they do all day?" I noticed many of the children looked forlorn. I had a sudden instinct to grab as many as I could and run out the door.

"We just watch them. They play in the backyard. If their parents' stats are up, they can come and see their children for an hour or so after dinner."

"Do they sleep here?"

"Yes, most of them do." She showed me a room farther down the hall. In it were rows of cribs side-by-side, about a dozen in the small room. "Some of the Sea Org children stay here, and some are sent to a ranch in Mexico if their parents are going to be on a mission for a long time," she explained.

"But don't the parents miss their children?"

"Remember," she told me severely, "children are part of the second dynamic. The third dynamic, the group, is more important than the second. The rule in Scientology is 'the greatest good for the greatest number of dynamics.' Our main purpose in Scientology is to clear the planet. Remember that. Until the children can begin working for the group, they're downstats and can't be rewarded.

"Besides, Hubbard says children are just thetans in small bodies. They're just as responsible as adults. We have to get their ethics in, so we don't reward them until they can produce."

She led me into a back room, which contained a solitary playpen. In the playpen was a tiny baby girl, horribly deformed. Her face was grotesque and distorted, her body twisted. One leg was shorter than the other, and her arms were abnormally short and deformed.

"This is Lisa," Colleen informed me. "Her mother is on staff. She took LSD when she was pregnant." She bent over the edge of the pen and stroked the baby's head. The baby seemed to have trouble breathing, and her eyes were clouded.

"She's blind, but she can hear you. We just talk to her and hold her, but I don't think she'll live long." She picked up the poor creature and handed her to me.

I spent the rest of the day holding and walking with baby Lisa. I tried to make contact with some of the other children as I walked around. They crowded around me, desperate for attention.

At the end of the day, I left the building and walked home, numb with shock. From then on, whenever I received any money from home or had anything left from my meager Sea Org pay, I walked to the drugstore on Alvarado Street and bought cheap children's books or crayons for the children of the Cadet Org.

I returned to the Cadet Org several days later for another shift at babysitting and learned that Lisa died two days earlier.

Another interesting experience in Scientology was my first payday. In Scientology, there's the practice known as "graphing one's stats." For every post in Scientology, there's an assigned statistic. For example, the statistic, or stat, for an Ethics Officer might be the number of ethics "cycles" handled hourly. The statistic for a "letter registrar," the person who wrote letters to the public, might be the number of letters written per hour. The stat for a student might be the number of points on course per hour. Each activity in every Scientology course was awarded a certain number of points.

Scientologists graph their stats by the hour, day, and week. Each Thursday, promptly at 2:00 PM, every Scientology staff member has to turn in his or her stats for the week to the division of the organization known as Inspection and Reports, or "I&R." Then each staff member is assigned a "condition" for that week. The staff member must apply the appropriate formula during the following week to move to a higher condition and better his stats.

Theoretically, a staff member in Scientology is expected to better his stats each week. If he doesn't, he'll be assigned to a "lower condition," which he then must "work out of" by performing even more work, sometimes of a menial and demeaning nature.

On Friday, after all the stats for the week have been tabulated, staff members who are not in a lower condition for the week receive their pay. The pay is calculated as follows: First, the gross income for the week for that particular org is computed. 10% of the GI is siphoned off the top to be paid to World Wide, the international headquarters of Scientology in Europe. At least, that was a practice during the years I was in Scientology. Then the expenses of the organization for that week are paid. The remaining money is allocated to payroll and is paid out according to a "units system."

Each job, or post, in Scientology is allocated a certain number of points, or units, with executive positions earning more points, while more menial jobs such as switchboard operator earn less points. The net income for the org is allocated to the staff in that org in proportion to the units for each post. In my post, as a Dianetics auditor in training—my unofficial post as an aide to Aileen not being recognized for the purposes of pay—I had a fairly minimal number of units.

On payday, Friday, we lined up outside the center and waited for the Director of Finance to arrive with our pay. A mobile canteen unit drove into the parking lot to take advantage of our weekly affluence. I waited in anticipation for my first Scientology pay. Having been without income for some time, I had a list of priorities to satisfy with my pay, ranging from toothpaste to an unaccustomed dinner out at a local diner with fellow staff members.

Finally, the finance person appeared with a box of small brown envelopes. Names were called one by one. I waited eagerly. I had worked hard my first week in the Sea Org, an average of sixteen to eighteen hours a day for seven days, with two-and-a-half hours off on Saturday for personal time.

Finally, my name was called. I reached for my envelope. I opened it and found a receipt and money enclosed for $2.11. I stared in disbelief. Had there been a mistake? I went to the finance officer.

"I got only $2.11," I stammered to the uniformed officer.

He took the receipt and checked the figures. "No. That's right. It was a slow week. According to your units, that's the correct pay. Maybe next week will be better." He handed me the receipt.

I walked away feeling deflated. My plans for shopping and dinner with friends faded into the sunset. I looked at the canteen, walked over, then selected a sandwich and can of soda.

"Two dollars." The canteen owner reached for the money.

Oh, well, I thought, handing him the money. *So much for payday.*

In the several years that I was to work for Scientology, the highest pay I ever remember receiving was $11.20.

"How do you survive?" I asked another girl who was on staff.

She looked at me and laughed. "Some of us work as topless dancers at night, after hours. It's the only way to get along on this pay."

Suddenly conscious of my chronically overweight body, I sighed. I would have to find another way to survive economically. I placed a collect call to my father. Maybe he could increase a small allowance he'd been sending to help me with my studies.

During the following weeks, I occasionally received a small check from my father that I cashed in the finance office. With those small windfalls, I could occasionally afford to go with the executives and more highly paid staff members to have dinner at the small diner right behind the LA Org. It was always a treat to enjoy the camaraderie of friends and the luxury of dining away from the staff house.

Mounted on the wall in the diner was a small black-and-white television. We usually arrived at the diner just a few minutes after six o'clock, just as the new science-fiction program *Star Trek* was being broadcast. I soon discovered that Scientologists watch the program from an entirely different perspective than did *wogs*. Wogs is the Scientology term for non-Scientologists, taken from an old English expression, an acronym for worthy Oriental gentleman, a derogatory term used to refer to the non-English natives of the British colonies.

"It's just old space opera," one staff member joked as we watched an episode. "They don't know it, but they're really just running their own track." To a Scientologist, track meant time track. The speaker meant that the events on the program were actually real events that happened long ago. The writers of *Star Trek* were just remembering events in their own distant past, events that were common to us all. To a Scientologist, that program had special relevance—it was our history.

The days in the Sea Org became weeks. Christmas passed. It seemed surreal to have warm weather on the day of that traditionally winter holiday. I discovered that Christmas was just another day in the week to Scientologists. As a Christian holiday, it had only token significance. We had a special buffet-style dinner served in the center. There were some cheeses in the center of the table that we were told that been sent expressly by Hubbard to reward us for our dedication and loyalty as staff members. I felt grateful.

After dinner, we returned to course. The rest of the day was just another day in the Sea Org.

One day soon after Christmas, Aileen asked the Course Supervisor to excuse me from course. I followed her into the office and saw a familiar figure sitting there.

"Dad!" I exclaimed in surprise. "What are you doing here?"

He shook my hand awkwardly. We weren't given to displays of affection in our family. He explained he was on business and decided to see my "school." I saw he carried his briefcase.

"Well, do you like it?" I asked expectantly.

"Everyone is certainly friendly," he said, glancing uncertainly at Aileen. "I was hoping I could take you out to dinner."

I looked at Aileen.

"Of course, dear. Go with your father and have a good time. I'll get you excused from course."

I took my dad to the diner, not knowing any other place nearby to eat. He looked worried.

"Your mother and I have been reading about this Scientology," he told me, taking newspaper clippings from his briefcase. "Here. I want you to read these."

I picked up a clipping from *Time*. The writer was obviously biased against Scientology and called it a cult.

"Scientology's not a cult," I informed my father. "It's just a group of people trying to make a difference in the world. This writer obviously didn't talk to anyone in Scientology, or he wouldn't have written these things." I returned the article.

"There are other articles." He handed me several more.

I look through them. The writers' orientation was obvious. "Dad, this is just *entheta.*" I remembered what Hubbard taught about this kind of journalism on one of his tapes. "That means it's against theta, or goodness. We're not supposed to read this stuff," I said coldly, pushing the articles back to his side of the table.

"Just read some of them," he pleaded.

"I don't need to read them. I know what they say without reading them. They're written by the suppressive press. These writers are paid by their bosses to write this stuff. They want to destroy Scientology, because it works. There are vested interests in this country who don't want to see Scientology expand. It's a threat to them, because they want to enslave people, and Scientology is in the business of freeing people." From my mouth came phrases I had heard over and over on Hubbard's training tapes.

"You're in a dangerous cult," my father argued. "We want you to quit this foolishness and come home. That's why I'm here. I've come to get you and take you home."

I stared at him in disbelief. He was beginning to sound like a Suppressive Person. A very unpleasant thought formed in my mind. Was it possible he was an SP?

"How does Mom feel about this?"

"She totally agrees. We both want you home. You can return to the university. If you come back now, you can still enroll for the spring semester." He looked at me hopefully.

"I don't want to come back. I don't want to go back to school. This is where I belong. I have a job here. I'm helping to Clear the planet. There's nothing on this whole planet more important than Scientology. These writers are wrong about Scientology. Scientology is the only hope on this planet that any of us have." I felt desperate. Could he force me to return home?

"No, you're wrong," he replied, sounding angry. "This Scientology is nonsense. You're in a cult, and I'm going to take you home. I want you to get your things and come with me. I have a ticket for you to come back to Michigan." He pulled a ticket from his pocket made out in my name.

I started crying. "Dad, I can't come back with you. I don't care what you think about Scientology. You just don't understand.

You can't tell me what to do anymore. I'm eighteen. Scientology is my life. I've signed a contract to work here, and I'm not leaving."

"What kind of contract?" he asked suspiciously.

"A Sea Org contract. I signed a contract to work for the Sea Org for a billion years. We're going to clear the planet. Then we're going to clear all the other planets in the universe. Scientology is the first chance in millions of years for us to be free. I'm not going to mess it up. There's nothing else in the world I want to do. How can I go back to music school when I have a chance here to help with something really important?"

He looked at me with a combination of exasperation and disbelief. "How can I get you to see the truth about what you're involved in? Can't you see the absurdity of what you're saying? A billion-year contract? Clearing the planet? This is nonsense. You need to come to your senses." He sounded very angry.

"Dad, I'm not coming back with you. I'll have dinner with you and talk to you, but I'm not coming back to Michigan. You can't make me." I wasn't about to give in.

He stared helplessly out the window. Then he turned and started speaking in a kinder, less-angry voice. "Look, I know we've never shown much affection in our family, but you know we love you. We care about you. Why do you think I came all the way out here to see you? We all care. Your brothers and sisters miss you, too. We all want you back home."

"What will you do if I don't come?"

"We'll try something to get you back. Legally. We'll fight. We'll sue this cult if we have to. We're not going to give you up to some harebrained cult."

Then I knew the truth. My father *was* an SP. Hubbard made it clear. I read all the teachings about the Suppressive Person on the course. The basic crime of Suppressive Persons was to attack Scientology, the only force for good and reason on the planet.

I read about this in the Ethics book. The Suppressive Person was also called the "antisocial personality," or the "anti-Scientologist." *There are certain characteristics and mental attitudes that cause about 20% of a race to oppose violently any betterment activity or group,* Hubbard wrote. He said such people cause untold trouble for betterment groups such as Scientology. *The antisocial personality supports only destructive groups and rages against and attacks any constructive or betterment group.*

Of course, I realized. *My father works for the government.*

According to Hubbard, the government was completely suppressive. His tapes told us all about the suppressive agencies and the federal government—the IRS, the FDA, the FBI, and the National Institute for Mental Health. The government, explained Hubbard, was a suppressive organization that controlled the country. The real truth was that behind the government was an invisible government that most people didn't know about. It consisted of a secret group of twelve extremely powerful men who were the real source of power in the world. They were particularly connected with the World Health Organization in Europe. They also pulled the strings that controlled the United States. People who worked for the government, like my father, were just minor suppressives who were attracted to that kind of work, because it was consistent with their inner, evil natures.

I stared at him in amazement. My eyes were being opened. I understood why there had been so much trouble in our family. My father was, as Hubbard put it, a "blazing SP."

"Look," I began, "I'm not coming home, and I don't want you to cause any trouble for Scientology. That would just get us both in trouble." I looked at him coldly and stood from the table. "I'm going back to the center. I can't stay here with you. I'm sorry you wasted your trip, but you did that on your own determinism, and I can't take responsibility for it." I was using more Scientology talk. Without looking back, I walked out the door.

I ran back to the center and burst into Aileen's office. "Aileen, my dad is threatening to sue Scientology. He says it's a cult. He wanted me to go back home with him." I was obviously upset.

She looked at me in concern. "Why? Tell me exactly what happened and what he said."

I related the entire event to her. She looked troubled.

"I'm afraid I'll have to write up a knowledge report about this. Your father could be a source of trouble for us. You'll have to work this out with Ethics. Until it's handled, I'm afraid you won't be able to go back on course. The first thing you need to do is go and report everything that happened to the MAA."

She pulled a routing form out of her top drawer. At the top it read, *Ethics Routing Form.*

Several minutes later, I sat in a chair opposite the teenage Ethics officer, telling him the same story I told Aileen.

"I'd like to indicate that your father is a Suppressive Person." He looked across the desk at me as if I were infected with a deadly virus. "The policy on suppressives is very clear." He handed me a policy letter written by Hubbard.

I read it carefully. According to Hubbard, the policy on suppressives was to "handle" or "disconnect."

"What does that mean?"

That was the wrong question. "What word don't you understand?" He looked at me with emotionless eyes.

"I understand the words. I just don't understand what I'm supposed to do."

"Very simple. Either you handle your father to the point where he's willing that you continue in the Sea Org, or you'll have to disconnect from him. You'll have to send him a disconnect letter."

"Disconnect letter?" That sounded ominous.

"Yes. I can help you write it. You'll tell him that you want no contact with him or the rest of your family now or at any point in the future. You'll formally disconnect from your suppressive family. Until you handle the situation one way or the other, you won't be allowed back on course. You're to report back to me at this time tomorrow."

The policy, I realized, was black and white, like everything else in Scientology. There was no room for feeling—not that I minded the lack of emotion with which this and similar situations were handled in Scientology. I had already done enough TR 0 bullbaited to not feel much about anything, but to tell my parents good-bye forever.... I squirmed inwardly at the thought.

I believed in the policy. I was already conditioned to believe that, if Hubbard said it, it must be right. I knew that Hubbard's way would always be the best and most rational solution, because he was the Source. In just a few short weeks, Hubbard already assumed occupancy of the place in my mind allocated to Father or Dad. He loved me, I believed, even more than my own father. He was father to us all.

I walked back to the house, having been barred from the course until the problem was resolved. I thought of my dad. He'd be home in a couple hours. I'd call him, and maybe he'd be more reasonable. Maybe he could be handled.

In my mind, the decision had already been made. My father was the enemy. I no longer thought of him as father. All those years I have been living with an SP without knowing it. That explained the conflict in my family. By virtue of being married to an SP, my mother was, by Scientology definitions, a PTS, or Potential Trouble Source. Both of them were endangering my Scientology career.

If they didn't agree to back off, I'd have to disconnect. I had to get back on course. Already my stats for the week were crashed, I thought dismally, wondering what Ethics condition I'd be assigned for the week.

I lay in my bed, thinking over all the years with my father. I thought of the twelve characteristics Hubbard listed in the Ethics book as being indicative of an SP.

> He or she speaks only in broad generalities.

Yeah, I thought, *Dad's always talking about "they this" and "they that."*

> Such a person deals mainly in bad news, critical remarks, invalidation, and general suppression.

Bull's eye, I thought. My father had a definite tendency to be critical. I thought of all the times he came home complaining about his coworkers, criticizing what they had done during the day.

> The antisocial personality alters, to
> worsen communication... passes on
> "bad news."

I thought of the times when my dad told us less-than-flattering stories about the people he worked with.

> He does not respond to treatment or
> psychotherapy.

Once, I remembered, my mother tried to get my dad into counseling to work on their marriage, but he refused to go.

> Surrounding such a personality we
> find cowed or ill associates who,
> when not driven actually insane, are
> yet behaving in a crippled manner in
> life, failing, not succeeding.

My mother's always sick, I thought. *What about my problems? My sister's always having trouble in school.*

I didn't need to read any further. There was no doubt in my mind. My dad was an SP, who was trying to interfere with my helping Scientology clear the planet. I felt angry.

I won't let him do this to me, I thought. *I'll get ethics in on my family. If I have to disconnect, then that's what I'll do.*

I waited for the hours to pass. I dreaded the call. Finally, I walked down to the convenience store a couple blocks away and placed the call.

My mother answered the phone and sounded cheerful. "Hi, dear. We were just thinking about you."

"Is Dad there?" I asked coldly. I knew what I was up against. My mother had no idea of the situation she was in, that she was PTS to a deadly SP.

"Yes. He just got in. I'm so disappointed that you didn't come back with him, but you need to know that we love you and will always be here for you."

"Could I just talk to Dad?"

He came on the line. "Margery, we won't give up without a fight. You tell Scientology they'll be hearing from my lawyer. I won't stand for this nonsense."

"OK, Dad. I'm sorry you feel that way. Tell Mom good-bye for me." I quickly hung up.

There's no going back now, I thought, walking back to the house, where I spent a sleepless night tossing in my bed, my sleep haunted with nightmares about my father. In one dream, he had a gun and stood outside the center, shooting through the windows.

The following morning, I walked to the center and went directly to the Ethics office.

"I need to disconnect from my family," I said calmly. "There's no hope of ever dealing rationally with my father. He's insane on the subject of Scientology. Hubbard was sure right about SPs. They hate what we're doing to save the planet. What do I have to do?" I looked across the table at the teenage Master at Arms.

"Here's what you have to write," he replied, handing me a blank sheet of paper and pen. He began to dictate. "I'm writing to notify you that I hereby disconnect from you." He paused. "I want no further contact with you at any time or under any circumstances. This decision is irrevocable."

I wrote exactly what he said.

"Now sign it," he commanded, handing me an envelope. "You can make this out, and we'll mail it for you."

I addressed the envelope.

"That's all there is to it," he said matter-of-factly. "I'll give you a form to get you back on course. You'll have to push to get your stats back up."

"I know. I'll do it. Thursday is still three days away."

I returned to the course room. *Just like that,* I thought. I tried to comprehend the fact that I'd never see or write my parents again. Somehow, it didn't seem real. I couldn't imagine life without Mom and Dad to fall back on.

I guess I'm on my own now. I know I did the right thing. I just wish I felt better about it.

For a moment, I had the fleeting thought to run back up the street to the store to call my dad and ask him for the ticket back home. I quickly pushed the thought aside. *Family,* I told myself, *is the second dynamic. The Sea Org is the third dynamic.* I repeated the phrase I was to hear many times in the coming years. "The greatest good for the greatest number of dynamics. Scientology must survive. My relationship with my family isn't important. All that's important is clearing the planet."

I can't think about them anymore, I told myself, as I approached the center. *They're no longer my family. Scientology is my family. This is my real home.*

I walked resolutely into the course room, more determined than ever to do well in Scientology.

I didn't think about my family again for a long time. I read the letters from my mother that arrived periodically at the center, but I threw them in the trash, feeling no emotion.

I passed my first initiation.

I was a real Scientologist.

CHAPTER NINE

Death on the Titanic

No sooner had I gone to sleep than I heard the early morning knock on my door. "0700. Time to get up."

I unwillingly forced open my eyes. *Get up,* I told myself, *or you'll fall back asleep.* I closed my eyes and snuggled down under the thin blanket to keep out the chill of the California winter night. *Just two minutes,* I bargained. For two minutes, the overwhelming temptation to sleep battled with the fear of Ethics. Finally, fear won out.

The previous night was an unusually late night. Two missionaries from the ship arrived the previous day at the center, dressed in starched dress whites with gold braided ropes hanging from their shoulders. At 11:00 PM, after the last of the public students drifted out the door following the customary sharing of our wins after class, the twenty-odd staff members from the center gathered in the front of the auditorium for a briefing by the missionaries.

"The tech is going in," they told us. "We're winning on every continent. The stats worldwide are in Affluence." That was a high Ethics condition. "We're getting Command Intention in all over the globe." That was what Ron wanted. "Clearing this planet becomes more a reality with each passing day."

Two new centers were established in South America during the past month, plus there was a new center in Germany, and an org in Italy. The stats for "raw meat PCs," or new people into Scientology, were almost double than at the same time the previous year.

They told stories about Ron and life aboard ship. Hubbard was doing his research on the upper OT levels, we learned. Although it had been a strenuous experience for him, he came through it shaken but alive. It was rumored that research into these levels was extremely hazardous, and anyone venturing into those areas prior to Hubbard met with death.

There were the customary rituals—the cheers to Ron, as we saluted his picture, the long ovations at each announcement of success, and the usual hard sell to all of us to push our stats even higher during the coming months.

They handed out stationery for each of us to write a personal letter to Ron, telling him about our wins and thanking him for his contribution to the survival of mankind.

It was 1:30 AM before the briefing was dismissed, and I walked wearily back to the house. I had no memory of going to bed.

Fatigue was a fact of life, a small sacrifice made by each of us daily to the exalted goal of planetary salvation. I didn't seem to dream anymore, I realized one morning. Sleep had become an experience in pure unconsciousness, much like the experience of being anesthetized for an operation. There was no longer any awareness of elapsed time between falling asleep and waking up in the morning.

An unfamiliar sound drifted into my consciousness, a soft, rhythmic tapping across the window. It was raining. It hadn't rained in weeks. I looked up at the somber sky that perfectly reflected my mood.

Fear permeated the outer limits of awareness. I had already had two warnings placed in my student file for being late to class, and the third one, I knew, would mean certain disciplinary action.

I reached for my sweater and walked slowly down the hall to the bathroom. The door was locked, and two people stood ahead of me in line. I accepted my fate and took my place behind a man I hadn't seen before. No one spoke. I assume everyone was too tired to attempt a morning greeting. Besides, I noticed Scientologists tended not to waste words. Communication was restricted to the functional, without the luxury of social niceties. Under the circumstances, I thought, somehow saying good morning seemed hypocritical.

House rules allotted us a strict three-minute limit on morning bathroom time. Showers had to be taken at breaks or during a time of less-critical bathroom demand. I splashed cold water on my face, trying to stimulate myself into consciousness.

The usual breakfast madness was in progress in the small kitchen, as an assorted two dozen or so inhabitants of the house scurried to make it to post or course before the strict eight o'clock deadline.

"Just coffee, please," I told Glenda, who currently served as kitchen I/C, in charge. "I managed to oversleep again. I'm starving, but I'll be late to course."

"Here." She handed me a slightly stale store-bought cinnamon roll. "You've still got a few minutes. Everyone's late this morning. Hubbard must've discovered a substitute for sleep. The missionaries were down here at 7:00 AM asking for breakfast. When I told them they'd have to wait, they put me in a condition of Liability. I already had too much to do today as it was," she grumbled.

"Yeah, but you don't argue with a missionary from the ship," Gerry looked up at his wife, "unless you're asking for trouble. I heard that they put the whole staff at the LA Org on beans and rice until they get their stats up. And they handed out seventy-two-hour amends projects to five of the execs. I saw them out in back of the org yesterday with gray rags around their arms, painting the annex. There were circles under their eyes, and they had beards. Three days with no sleep must be rough. They were a sorry lot." He chuckled.

I liked that couple. Gerry was a part-time character actor in Hollywood, and Glenda managed somehow to finagle the kitchen job, so she could care for her two-month-old son herself. Two months earlier, she delivered the baby in the front room across the hall, assisted only by Gerry and a midwife. I never witnessed a home birth before and was full of awe for Glenda.

"I wouldn't be on the ship for anything," remarked Jon, a quiet, uniformed, twenty-year-old from Denmark. He was a Class-8 Auditor, the highest trained person in the house and therefore respected. "I've heard they've been throwing people overboard every morning. Part of a new Ethics crackdown. They also put people down in the bilges for a week at a time. I'm just glad I'm here," he said gratefully.

"Why would they throw people overboard?" I asked incredulously. "That sounds dangerous."

"I guess they throw them a life preserver once they're in," he answered, gulping down the last of his coffee. "But it's dangerous. If you hit the strake on the side of the ship as you go under, you might as well kiss this life good-bye. I'd rather take my chances with good old LA smog." He set his cup in the sink and saluted as he headed out the door. "Later, everyone."

"Yeah. Me, too." I swallowed the last of the stale roll with a gulp of coffee. "I've got exactly thirty seconds to get my body into a chair next door. Thanks for the coffee, Glenda." I sprinted out the door and around the corner to the center.

I made it into my seat just as the Supervisor called her customary, "That's it. Start of course." She gave me a warning look. "That's cutting it close, Wakefield. Better get your ethics in."

I nodded and quickly immersed myself in my checksheet. With just a little more reading, I'd be able to audit. I looked in satisfaction at the pages I had filled with my initials, as I completed the items.

Aileen and Antonio had gone away on a mission together. They were rumored to be helping set up a new Celebrity Center in Canada. I felt abandoned when they left, but at least I'd be able to make lots of progress on the course while they were gone.

I turned to the next item on my check sheet, an essay entitled, *The Evolution of Man.*

> Man evidently began as a monocell, without intercellular relation problems. He

> developed by counterefforts to a degree that banded together many cells with one central control center. He joined with a second control center and dual-evolved organically into Man.
>
> The problems of the monocell by itself were strenuous but uncomplicated, having relationship only with the environment in its grossest form—pure MEST. These problems included such phenomena as the explosion of cosmic rays.

How is it, I wondered, *I can simultaneously understand and not understand everything that Hubbard writes?* I knew not to ask questions. That would only result in a word-clearing session in which I would have to look up every word in the bulletin while I was hooked up to an E-meter, a very tedious affair. I had learned by experience it was better to struggle in silence.

> The problems of a cellular colony under one control center were yet similar to those of the monocell. The protagonist had but one personality and one antagonist—MEST. Vegetable and invertebrate problems are found in this period.
>
> Interpersonal relations, when in difficulty, have their foot in the elementary problems of the dual-control problems, wherein the current control center confuses its ancient problems with its partner center with the problems the organism may have with other individuals in the environment.
>
> The evolution of Man presents many fascinating aspects, but all have basic

> simplicities. There are, essentially, only two sets of problems: The problems between the control center of the mind and the elements; the problem of the control center of the mind with its alternate control center.
>
> An auditor need only resolve, in any case, the essential basic confusions of the preclear in each of these two sets.

I wanted desperately to yawn but suppressed the urge. I read back through the section again, looking up the word *protagonist*. *It makes a kind of sense,* I thought, *I guess*. I initialed the appropriate space, indicating that I read the essay.

I look surreptitiously around the classroom. Two students were doing TR 0 in the far end of the room, while two others had started their bullbaiting. One pretended an English accent.

"I say, Old Chap," he said, clapping his partner's shoulder, "do y'know where I could git a bit o' arse? It's been a bloody long time."

His partner smiled.

"Flunk for smiling. Start!" He said sternly. "I say, Old Chap," he began again.

My friend Kris was absorbed in an elaborate clay demo. Two other students were listening to tapes. Another eighteen people studied silently at the two long tables where I sat.

I began to fantasize about being in bed, snug under my blanket, and of being able to sleep just once for as long as I wanted. I remembered rainy mornings at school when my earliest class was at 10:00 AM, and I'd been able to sleep in until 9:00. As I thought back, it seemed an unbelievable luxury.

My head jerked back. I actually started falling asleep. I dug my fingernails into my palms, willing myself into consciousness. I turned the page in my check sheet and read, *History of Man*, a book by Hubbard. I turned to the foreword and began to read.

> This is a cold-blooded and factual account of your last 60 trillion years.

I blinked and looked again. Yes, that's what it said. I continued reading.

> The test of any knowledge is its usefulness. Does it make one happier and more able? By it and with it, can he better achieve his goals?
>
> This is useful knowledge. With it the blind again see, the lame walk, the ill recover, the insane become sane, and the sane become saner. By its use, the thousand abilities man has sought to recover become his once more.
>
> Gravestones, ancient vital statistics, old diplomas, and medals will verify in every detail the validity of "many lifetimes." Your E-meter will tell you.

As I read, I discovered the book was divided between a description of the events in the past "track" of the "genetic entity," and the events in the past track of thetan, or soul. The genetic entity referred to those incidents that were supposedly recorded at a cellular level in the person's body. The events of the theta being were the memories of the person himself as a soul.

According to Hubbard, some of the past events that are common to all of us on a cellular level were:

> The Atom. The very first stage of being a physical life, described by Hubbard as "a condition of motion, with the preclear in the center, with rings of motion traveling around him."

The Cosmic Impact, in which "cosmic rays enter the body in large numbers and occasionally explode in the body."

The Photon Converter, in which we, as algae and plankton begin "taking their living from photons from the sun and minerals in the sea."

The Helper, which is "mitosis, or cell splitting," in which one half of the split cell tries to help the other half survive.

The Clam, which when restimulated in a person may cause problems in the opening and closing of the jaw.

The Weeper, a bivalve, and the first creature to use the land. An important stage in our evolution. The Weeper later develops into the eyes of the person, and the pumping out of salt water in the Weeper is the basic reason why we cry.

Further stages in our evolutionary past included the Birds, Being Eaten, The Sloth, the Ape, Piltdown Man, and the Caveman.

In contrast were the past events in the history of the theta being.

The Jack in the Box. "An invader trick, a method of trapping thetans." A thetan was given a box of pictures, and "when he replaces the lid, the box explodes violently." Hubbard said that people with that incident in restimulation were very curious about cereal boxes.

The Halver. "A half-light, half-black gun that shot out a wave. Half of the wave, usually the black, hit the right side of the victim's body; the other half, in the same explosion, usually the light side, hit the left side of the victim. "The Halver was rigged up with religious symbols, and it truly lays in religion."

Facsimile One. An incident in everyone's bank, or reactive mind, originally laid down in this galaxy about one million years ago. In it, "a push-pull wave is played over the preclear, first on his left side, then on his right and back and forth from side to side, laying in a bone-deep somatic. When this treatment is done, the preclear is dumped in scalding water, then immediately in ice water. Then the preclear is put in a chair and whirled around."

Hubbard claimed when that incident is run, or audited out, it would eradicate "such things as asthma, sinus trouble, chronic chills, and a host of other ills."

Before Earth. An incident in which the thetan is "summoned before a council, is frowned upon, and then sent elsewhere than where he is." The effect is to make the person a "more obedient colonist."

The Joiner, in which "a person is 'packed in' with other souls by electronics."

The Ice Cube, in which "the being is packed in ice, taken to a new area, and is usually dumped in the ocean." When that incident is in restimulation, the person may suffer from chronically cold hands and feet.

Between Lives. The familiar between-lives implants. In this incident, the person

> "'reports in,' is given a strong forgetter implant, and is then shot down to a body just before it is born."

About those implants, Hubbard wrote, *The report station for most has been Mars. Some women report to stations elsewhere in the solar system. There are occasional incidents about Earth report stations. The report stations are protected by screens. The last Martian report station was established in the Pyrenees.*

> The Emanator. "This is a large, glowing body of radioactive material which hangs magically in thin air, a sort of god and all-knower. Its outpulse puts one into a trance."

I was getting a headache. I looked up from my book and around at the class. I wanted to ask someone about what I was reading, but I would have to wait for break, when I was safely outside the ever-present scrutiny of the Supervisor.

The other incidents on the theta track, I continued reading, were the Double Body, Theta Traps, the Bodybuilder, the Jiggler, the Whirler, the Bouncer, the Spinner, the Rocker, the Boxer, the Faller, the Education, and the Fly Trap.

On that last, Hubbard wrote:

> It was of a gummy material. The thetan who got into it punched and fought at this material until he was psychotic enough to react to the physical-universe laws of responding to motion. He was taken out of this trap by a crew of do-gooders who caught him for his own good and who trained him in religious sweetness and syrup until they considered him fit to be part of their group.

I closed the book and looked around the room. Kris was sitting across from me at the table. The Supervisor was at her desk, occupied with paperwork. I knew we weren't allowed to talk on course unless we were doing a checkout. To be caught talking might mean a pink sheet to Ethics.

I reached over and tapped Kris' study pack. When she looked up, I held up *History of Man*, so she could see the title.

"Did you read this?" I whispered.

"Yeah," she whispered back.

"What did you think of it? Is he for real?"

She nodded. "Yeah, I guess. I thought it was pretty weird, too. I figure it's probably just some kind of analogy or symbolism or something."

"But what if he's really serious about this stuff? I mean, I knew we were supposed to come from apes, but I have trouble believing I was once a clam."

"It might have something to do with the upper levels." She looked around furtively for the Supervisor.

"It's OK. She's doing paperwork at her desk. I just feel confused. I know Hubbard is Source. I believe what he says is true, but this stuff is wild."

"Maybe there's some reason he had for writing it that we don't know about. Anyway, I decided the only thing that's important is the auditing. The tech works. When you start auditing, you'll see."

The Supervisor looked up from her desk and surveyed the class. I quickly looked down at my pack and signaled Kris to stop talking.

I wish Antonio were here, I thought wistfully. *I know he could explain this to me. He always knows the answer to everything.* I made a mental note to ask him about the book, as soon as he returned to the center.

The next few days on the course, I learned to use the E-meter. Since I didn't have a meter of my own, I already arranged with Antonio to use his while he was away. Eventually, I would have to somehow come up with the money to buy my own meter.

During the E-meter drills, I learned how to keep the needle on the dial by moving the Tone Arm to compensate for the needle swings off the dial. I learned how to correctly set the sensitivity knob for each person I was auditing, as different people might have different sensitivities to the meter. People who didn't "read" well on the meter required a higher sensitivity setting than those who did.

Another part of my E-meter training consisted of learning to differentiate among the various different types of "reads." When the needle swung sharply to the right, it was known as a "fall." That was a sign that electrical charge was "coming off the PC's case." In other words, they were discharging unwanted mental tension.

A very long fall to the right was known as "a long fall blowdown." Other falls could be either "short falls" or "long falls." The differences in the reads were significant to the auditor. A rise meant that the person being audited was actually "keying in" or accumulating mental mass. His "case" was becoming more solid. If a person's "TA" or Tone Arm setting was too high at the start of the session, that meant that he or she had something in restimulation and might need to go through a "review session" before being audited on the current action to find out what he was upset about.

Other reads of the needle included a "theta bop," which was a rapid back-and-forth motion of the needle; a "rock slam," a distinct read that usually indicated that the person being audited had "evil purposes" or was an SP; and a "dirty needle," a jagged, irregular motion of the needle that usually meant the preclear had "withholds" or that he was withholding something from the auditor.

I practiced with the E-meter for several days, running make-believe sessions with a large doll propped in the chair across from me until I was completely comfortable with using the very precise Dianetic commands while simultaneously handling the E-meter.

Finally, I was ready to audit my first preclear.

I was assigned to audit Tommy, another student on the course. He was an artist who wrote poetry, illustrated by detailed and intricate line drawings done with a very fine black pen. He was very popular at the center, and I felt honored to be his auditor.

We walked back to the house where I had reserved one of the two small rooms upstairs used for auditing. I already had the table set up with the E-meter ready in the middle. On my side of the table were the paper and pens I would use to keep a running log of the session to be submitted to the C/S, the Case Supervisor, after the session.

We sat across from each other. Tommy reached for the small V-8 cans connected to the leads attached to the meter. He smiled at me.

"Have you had plenty of rest?" I asked. It was necessary to make sure the preclear had plenty of rest and wasn't hungry before starting the session.

He nodded.

"Are you hungry?"

"Nope."

"All right. This is the session," I announced, writing down the starting time of the session on my worksheet.

The beginning of the session was easy. I had to ask him a series of questions from a sheet printed in green called, appropriately, a Green Form. The answers of the preclear to the questions on the form would determine what to "run" in the session.

As we completed the form, Tommy revealed that he recently suffered from headaches in which he felt a sharp pain behind his eyes. That turned out to be the correct item to run.

I looked at him with my very best TR 0. "Locate an incident containing a sharp pain behind your eyes," I commanded.

He closed his eyes. "OK."

"Good. When was it?"

"Yesterday. On course. I had a headache."

"All right. How long did it last?"

"About three hours. Most of the afternoon. I felt nauseous, too."

"OK. Move to the beginning of the incident and tell me when you are there."

"I'm there." His eyes were still closed.

"OK. Scan through to the end of the incident."

After a long silence, he said, "OK."

"All right. Tell me what happened."

"I was sitting in class, and I started to get the same kind of headache I've been having lately. It feels like a shooting pain behind my eyes. I was having trouble seeing right. I was sick to my stomach, too."

I had him visualize the incident again, then asked him if the picture was receding or becoming more solid.

"Solid."

"OK. Is there an earlier, similar incident containing a sharp pain behind the eyes?" I waited while he mentally searched for another picture.

After a couple of minutes, he recalled another headache several days earlier. We ran that according to the same procedure.

All auditing had to be very precisely done. Any deviation from the exact procedure written down by Hubbard was known as "squirreling" and was an Ethics offense. Continued squirreling would result in expulsion from Scientology and being declared a Suppressive Person.

After going through several similar memories Tommy had of headaches in this lifetime, I asked him for yet another earlier incident.

He was silent for a long time. "Well, I don't know. I seem to be looking at a picture of a grassy field."

"All right. When was it?"

"About 1,600 years ago." He opened his eyes.

"How long did it last?"

"Not long. About half an hour." He closed his eyes again.

The incident turned out to be a time when he was a monk in ancient Italy. His eyes were put out for heretical beliefs.

After going through that incident, I asked if there was an earlier one. I was beginning to wonder when we were going to reach the end of the session. It was rumored that sessions sometimes lasted for eight to ten hours or longer.

Tommy located an earlier incident, several million years ago. A metal band was put around his head that was slowly squeezed tighter and tighter, causing a sharp pain in his head.

Finally, at the end of that incident, Tommy opened his eyes and began smiling. "Maybe that's why I've been getting all these headaches," he said hopefully. "All this reading about all these implants must have been keying in my headaches. That's really neat. Maybe now they'll stop."

"Great." I smiled back at him. "I'd like to indicate to you that your needle is floating. End of session."

He put down the cans and stretched. "That felt good." He yawned. "Thanks a lot."

I turned off the meter and told Tommy he could go over to the Examiner, as I had to write up the session's final report. It was necessary for the preclear to visit the Examiner after each session. The Examiner would check his TA, tone arm position, and needle action after the session, to make sure that he had a floating needle and that the session went well. The Examiner's report was part of the paperwork that had to be submitted to the C/S.

I wrote up the session, filling out a session cover sheet, carefully noting down the Tone Arm position at the end of the session and the ending time.

I walked to the center to pick up the exam report and turn in my folder to the C/S. *What a relief,* I thought. Everything went the way it was supposed to. I happily anticipated the "Very Well Done" I would get from the C/S. All sessions were graded in that manner.

I return to class and gave Kris a thumbs-up sign. "It was easy," I told her.

"See? I told you. Wait till you do more. It's a blast," she whispered.

We returned to our reading.

The following day, I audited Tommy on his "feeling of nausea." The "basic" incident on this "chain" turned out to be another implant millions of years ago when he was being spun around in some kind of device while subjected to electronic beams. I turned in that session and received my second "Very Well Done." I felt proud.

    I reported to the center for my third and, hopefully, last auditing session. If the session was successful, I would graduate from the course. I'd be a full-fledged Hubbard Standard Dianetic Auditor, able to audit "paying PCs" and help make money for the center.

    I walked to the Supervisor's desk for my next assigned preclear. A young boy sat in a chair beside her desk.

    "This is David, your preclear," the Supervisor announced without looking up.

    The boy stood and looked at me shyly. "My parents brought me here. They're in the Sea Org. I have a problem with wetting my bed. They said you were going to help me."

    Although surprised, I managed to smile. "How old are you, David?"

    "Eight."

    I looked at the Supervisor uncertainly. "How can I audit someone who's only eight years old?"

    "Where in the tech did it say that you couldn't audit someone that age?" she asked icily.

    "Nowhere, I guess, but...."

    "I suggest you get your ethics in," she said sternly, "and take your preclear into session."

    I looked down at David. "Well, OK. Come on, David. Let's go see what happens."

    He walked silently beside me on the way to the house.

    "How long have your parents been in the Sea Org?"

    "As long as I can remember. I think since I was a baby. My older sister is in the Commodore's Messenger Org on the ship. She sends me postcards."

    I heard about the group of teenage girls and boys who served as Hubbard's personal aides on the ships. According to the rumors, they were being groomed for executive positions in the organization.

"How about you, David? Do you go to school?"

"I go to the Scientology school. We learn TRs and all sorts of things. In four more years, I'll be old enough to join the Sea Org, too. I'm going to work on the ship and be a famous auditor. I'll get to travel all over the world." He kicked a stone on the sidewalk.

"Do you get to see your parents a lot?"

"Sometimes. When they're here. A lot of the time, they're gone. Mostly, I stay with the other kids in a house by the AO. That's where my parents work when they're here." He looked up at me. "Is it OK for you to audit me?" he asked anxiously.

"Yes, I guess so. Have you had auditing before?"

"Oh, yes. Lots of times. Sometimes, my dad audits me. Whenever I get sick, I get a session. Or when I have to get my ethics in," he said matter-of-factly.

We reached the house. As I hung the *In Session, Do Not Disturb* sign on the outside and closed the door, David sat at the table and picked up the cans. He sat patiently waiting for me to start the session.

I asked him the preliminary questions about sleep and food. "OK, David," I said, adjusting the meter. "This is the session."

I did an assessment to see what somatics were associated with his wetting the bed. "A wet feeling" turned out to be the largest reading item.

"Locate an incident containing a wet feeling," I said gently.

He immediately closed his eyes. *He's done this before,* I realized.

In response to my questions, he remembered several times in the past when he wet the bed, each one happening earlier in time. I asked him for an even-earlier incident. His eyes closed, he seemed to be concentrating.

"I see a ship," he said. "People are running all over. They're screaming."

"When was it?" I asked calmly.

"A long time ago. It was before I was born. About fifty years ago, I guess."

"How long did it last?"

"It lasted a couple hours. The ship is sinking. Everyone's running around and screaming."

I took him through the incident using the exact commands I was taught. "Tell me what happened," I said.

He sat quietly with his eyes closed. "I'm in this little room. I'm in a crib. There's water coming up around me. I'm getting wet. I hear people screaming in the halls. I wonder where my parents are. Pretty soon, the water comes all the way up over my head." He opened his eyes and looked at me sadly. "I was a little baby on the ship, and I drowned. I think it was the *Titanic*."

"All right," I acknowledged. "Is there an earlier incident?"

"No. Just that one," he said decisively. "I was a baby on the *Titanic*, and I drowned."

I took him through the incident again.

"That's all there is. It was me. My parents went away and left me in this room on the *Titanic*, and I drowned."

One of the inviolable rules of the Auditor's Code was to never invalidate a preclear's data, so I ended the session.

David smiled at me. "Does this mean I won't ever wet my bed again?"

"I guess we'll just have to wait and see." I didn't want him to sense the doubts I had. "Let's go back to the center, and you can see the Examiner."

A few minutes later, David sat in the chair near the Supervisor, waiting for one of the teenage guides at the Org to come and walk him back home. I sat in the course room and watched as he left, holding the young aide's hand. I felt vaguely uneasy about something, but I didn't know what. I waited for the C/S to return to my session.

Half an hour later, the Supervisor called out in a loud voice, "That's it, Everyone. Margery just passed the Dianetics Course. She's now a Hubbard Standard Dianetic Auditor!"

Immediately, there was applause from the class. I stood and knew I would have to make the obligatory speech.

"It was a lot easier than I thought it would be," I said, trying to say something positive and not give away the misgivings I felt inside. "I know I have a lot of exciting sessions ahead. I look forward to being an auditor and helping Clear the planet." I sat down to more applause.

The Supervisor came over. "Your next step is Success." She handed me a pink sheet on which she had printed my name and the words *Routing Form to Success.*

I walk down the hall to a door with a sign that read, *Success and Certificates.*

I knocked. Beverly, a very large woman and one of the staff workers at the center, handed me a piece of paper with a picture at the top of a dove flying through clouds. At the top of the paper were the words in large blue script, *Success Story.*

"Fill this out," she instructed me. "You have to do this after you finish each course."

"What happens if someone doesn't want to fill it out?"

"Then they have to go back on course to see what they didn't understand," she replied. "If they're not happy with the course, it means they had a M/U (misunderstood word) somewhere on the course. They can't graduate until they find it."

"Oh. I just wondered." I looked down at the paper and began writing. *I had some wins on this course. The auditing was easier than I thought. I feel good knowing I can help people with their problems.*

I returned the paper to Beverly.

"OK. You're all finished here. You can pick up your certificate later this afternoon. Now you'll be ready to route onto your next course. I'll take you down to the Registrar." With some difficulty, she got up out of her chair.

Within ten minutes, I was signed up and given my study packs for the next course—Level 0.

I was on my way. *At this rate*, I thought optimistically, *I'll probably make Class 6 within one year*. When I returned to my chair, no one looked up.

Later that afternoon, I returned to Success to retrieve my certificate. It looked very impressive. My name had been printed in gold script. An official-looking seal was stamped and imprinted with the date. I looked with satisfaction at the tangible proof of my first achievement as a Scientologist.

Many years later, back home in Michigan, I would spread all my hard-won Scientology certificates out on the bed. They looked so official. Unfortunately, as I was to learn on a cold February day twelve years later, in the "wog world," my certificates had absolutely no value.

One night, I took all the certificates and burned them one by one in a fire my dad built in the living room fireplace. It was a hard lesson in relative cultural values.

I never saw young David again. Occasionally, I thought of him and wondered if he still wet his bed.

I never found out.

CHAPTER TEN

Find Out Who You Really Are

Hours became days, the days became weeks, and the weeks evolved inevitably into months. Scientology in Los Angeles, in stark contrast to the seediness of its surroundings, was prospering. Each week, new celebrities from Hollywood were lured into the life at Celebrity Center. Studios for artists were sectioned off in the front part of the building. The auditorium on Monday and Thursday evenings became the setting for the popular "Poetry and Coffee by Candlelight" talent shows. The stats, we were informed at the weekly Monday morning staff briefings, were rising steadily week after week.

I suffered through and survived my first hot and smoggy LA summer. Noxious poisons, mixed into the morning mists, hung in the air, becoming more concentrated as the day wore on, turning the simple act of breathing into a difficult, disagreeable experience.

Antonio and Aileen had since returned to the center, and my family life was again complete. Nestled in the comfortable womb of Scientology, surrounded by the extended family of the staff at the center, I happily enjoyed the moratorium from maturity and reality called life.

A few things changed. Because of an influx of new staff members, I was required to move to a different staff house on nearby Beacon Street, a house in which the general standard of living was greatly inferior to anything I ever experienced. I was allocated a lumpy mattress on the floor in the large front room, with a ragged blanket for covering. A network of clotheslines was strung throughout the room to separate the quarters of the married couples in the back of the room from those of us who were single in the front. The house was infested with roaches, and I found them crawling on the walls of the shower when I bathed in the evening.

The hardships of life served only to add nobility to the cause. The Sea Org, Hubbard told us repeatedly in his tapes, was the elite of planet Earth. One day soon, we'd come into our rightful inheritance of true honor, recognition, and material reward.

Sometime in the early 1970s, Scientology became a church.

"A church?" I asked a friend who worked in the Guardians Office, the notorious private CIA-like branch of Scientology. "Why?"

"It's just a tax matter," he assured me. "It won't really change the way anything works. It's just a way to deal with this oppressive government."

I was satisfied with that explanation. It was consistent with the policy from Ron that came out soon afterward in which he said, "Scientology 1970 is being planned on a religious-organization basis throughout the world. This will not upset in any way the usual activities of the organization. It is entirely a matter for accountants and solicitors."

Everyone on staff was required to become a minister in the Church of Scientology, and we were given exactly one week to do so. The list of qualifications to become a minister of Scientology was given in an early policy by Hubbard.

> Must have a validated certificate in Scientology.
> Must know the Church Creed verbatim.
> Must be capable of giving the various ceremonies.
> Must be able to pass an examination of the great religions.
> Must have a knowledge of St. John.
> Must be of good moral character.
> Must be able to conduct a Sunday service for the Church.
> Must have moral and ethical codes by which he can live and abide.

To fulfill requirement number four, I was given a book to read entitled, *Great Religions of the World.*

I had seen Antonio perform the Scientology christening ceremony many times at the center. It was very informal. Hubbard gave a sample of a christening ceremony at one of his early congresses. It went something like this:

> (Hubbard) "OK. The parents of the child will bring him front and center."
>
> (To the audience) "This is John and Anne Smith. James and Susie Baker have decided to become godparents."
>
> (To the child) "Here we go. How are you? All right. Your name is Zachary Smith. You got that? Good. There you are. Did that upset you? Now do you realize that you're a member of the HASI (Hubbard Association of Scientologists International)? Pretty good, huh?
>
> "All right. I want to introduce you to your father. This is Mr. Smith. Here's your mother.
>
> "And now, in case you get into trouble and want to borrow some quarters, here's Mr. Baker. See him? He's your godfather. Take a look at him. That's right. Here is Susie Baker in case you want a real good auditor. Got it?
>
> "Now you're suitably christened. Don't worry about it. It could be worse. OK. Thank you very much. They'll treat you all right."

Antonio did his christenings pretty much like that. On the minister's course, I didn't have much trouble reciting that or the other church ceremonies. I passed the course easily within one week, became a full-fledged minister, and promptly forgot the whole thing.

Whatever convictions I previously held about religion were quickly overturned in Scientology. In his tapes and bulletins, Hubbard took frequent digs at Christianity. Like all Scientologists, I believed Hubbard to be an incarnation of Buddha. Didn't he say so in his poem, *The Hymn of Asia?*

> Everywhere you are
>
> I can be addressed
>
> But in your temples best
>
> Address me and you address
>
> Lord Buddha
>
> Address Lord Buddha
>
> And you then address
>
> Meitreya

On the tapes, Hubbard frequently told us that 2,500 years ago in the Vedas, Buddha predicted that in 2,500 years he would come again to earth as a red-haired religious leader. Who else, concluded Hubbard, could it be?

Much later, on one of the advanced courses, I learned the "truth" about Jesus Christ. Hubbard was talking about implants at the time.

> Somebody on this planet around 600 BC
> found some pieces of R6 (an implant).
>
> I don't know how they found it; either by
> watching madmen or something. But since

> that time they have used it. And it became what is known as Christianity.
>
> The man on the cross. There was no Christ!
>
> The Roman Catholic Church, through watching the dramatizations of people, picked up some little fragments of R6.

In another bulletin, Hubbard announced that he had been to heaven three times. Heaven, of course, was just another implant.

> For a long while, some people have been cross with me for my lack of cooperation in believing in a Christian heaven, God, and Christ. I have never said I didn't believe in a Big Thetan, but there was something very corny about heaven et al. Now I have to apologize. There was a heaven. Not too unlike, in cruel betrayal, the heaven of the Assassins in the 12th century, who, like everyone else, dramatized the whole track implants.
>
> Yes, I've been to heaven. So have you. You have the pattern of its implants in the HCO Bulletin Line Plots (Hubbard's diagrams of implants). It was complete with gates, angels, and plaster saints—and electronic implantation equipment. So there was a heaven after all—which is why you are on this planet and were condemned never to be free again until Scientology.

The only difference I noticed in the center after we became a religion was that someone tacked up a small sign over the back room in the center that read, *Chapel*. On Sunday evenings, one of the staff members who was designated the Chaplain held a short service in the chapel. The sermon usually centered on some aspect of Scientology that was helpful to mankind.

One day, I complained to Aileen that it was many months since I had been given any auditing, although I did the TRs routinely with other staff members.

As usual, Aileen quickly remedied this.

"Margery?"

I was relaxing on the walk in the parking lot on my midmorning break. I looked up to see one of the students on the course, a tall, slim Spanish boy, named Louis. Like most of the other students, he was in an aspiring actor. I looked up at him.

"Yeah?"

"How would you like to get audited on your grades?"

"Really?" I was immediately interested.

"Yes. Come with me."

He led me into the course room and took me to the back of the room where a large chart, printed in red, hung on the wall. The chart read in big letters, *The Bridge to Total Freedom*. It was, I knew, the map to all the levels in Scientology.

"You're here." He pointed to a level near the bottom that read *Dianetics Completion*. "I'm going to audit you up to here." He ran his hand about one-third of the way up the chart.

I moved forward to read the tiny letters on the chart. The first level read, *Grade 0*. Under the *Ability Gained* column it read, *Ability to Communicate Freely with Anyone on Any Subject*.

"I don't think I could ever do that." I looked at Louis in discouragement. "I've never been very good at talking to people. I just never know what to say."

"Don't worry. You'll get there. I promise. That is, if you want to try."

"Sure." I looked at him eagerly. "When do we start?"

"How about right now?" He looked at me and smiled.

We walked to his tiny apartment a few blocks away. His E-meter was already set up in the middle of the table.

I sat and picked up the cans. He asked if I was tired or hungry.

"No. I'm fine."

"All right. I'm going to audit you on Grade 0 or Communication." He looked across at me with shining, dark-black eyes and perfect TR 0. "OK. Who are you willing to talk to?"

I looked at him. "Who?"

He didn't answer.

"You mean just anyone? Anyone I could talk to?"

He didn't blink. "I'll repeat the auditing question," he said gently. "Who are you willing to talk to?"

I sat back in my chair and thought. "I guess I can talk to my mother." I looked at him.

"Good. Now, who else are you willing to talk to?"

"Who else?" I paused. "My father."

"OK. Who else are you willing to talk to?"

"Antonio."

"Good. Who else are you willing to talk to?"

"Aileen."

"OK. Who else are you willing to talk to?"

"Kris."

"Good. Who else are you willing to talk to?"

"Beverly. I can talk to Beverly."

"Good. Who else are you willing to talk to?" He still hadn't moved or blinked in the whole time he had been asking me the question.

"I don't know. I guess anyone in the center."

"OK. Who else are you willing to talk to?"

"Well, I guess I'd be willing to talk to you." I looked across at him. *What am I supposed to do here?* I wondered. I was getting the idea that I was supposed to come to some kind of realization.

"All right. Who else are you willing to talk to?"

"The mailman." I liked the friendly older man who delivered the mail at the center every morning.

"Good. Who else are you willing to talk to?"

I began to feel annoyed. I was just supposed to sit there and answer the question over and over? "Louis, am I supposed to think of something different? I don't understand the point of this."

"OK. I'll repeat the auditing question. Who else are you willing to talk to?"

OK, I thought. *If this is what he wants to do, I'll show him I can hold out as long as he can.* "The Course Supervisor."

"Good. Who else are you willing to talk to?"

"The Ethics Officer."

"OK. Who else are you willing to talk to?"

"The mayor of Los Angeles."

"Good. Who else are you willing to talk to?"

"The queen of England." I felt hostile.

"OK. Who else are you willing to talk to?"

"The President of the United States."

"All right. Who else are you willing to talk to?"

"Jesus Christ."

"OK. Who else are you willing to talk to?"

"Mickey Mouse."

"OK. Who else are you willing to talk to?"

"Donald Duck."

"Good. Who else are you willing to talk to?"

I was starting to get really mad. "Louis," I pleaded. "Could we stop this? I don't know what to tell you. I don't know what you want. I'm getting frustrated."

He looked at me with his melting eyes, but there was no change in his expression. "I'll repeat the auditing question. Who else are you willing to talk to?"

"Oh, I don't know. I *can* talk to anyone. Anyone. What else can I tell you? Clark Gable, Bette Davis, Marilyn Monroe, Robin Hood, Zorro, Bugs Bunny, my sister, L. Ron Hubbard. Anyone. I can talk to anyone."

He didn't reply and just watched me.

"That's it, isn't it?" I started laughing. "That's what I'm supposed to say. Well, it's true. I can talk to anyone. I just never realized it before."

He looked at the meter. "I'd like to indicate that your needle is floating," he said with a smile.

We walked back to the Examiner.

"This is wild, Louis. Just by asking a question over and over you can get someone to realize things? I can't wait for the rest of the Levels."

Within half an hour, we were back in session. Louis began the process.

"What are you willing to talk to me about?"

"To you? I could talk to you about Scientology."

"OK. What else are you willing to talk to me about?"

"About your mother and father."

"Good. What else are you willing to talk to me about?"

"The weather."

"OK. What else are you willing to talk to me about?"

"Louis, I get it. I know the answer. I can talk to you about anything," I said in excitement, realizing I believed what I was saying.

"Good." He looked down at the meter.

"Don't tell me. I already know. My needle is floating." I looked at him and laughed.

He turned off the meter, and we returned to the center. He told me to wait in the chair in the course room.

Fifteen minutes later, the Supervisor called out, "That's it! Margery has just become a Grade 0 Release!"

"It was funny," I said in my speech. "It wasn't what I expected, but it worked."

I was given an Attestation of Release form to sign. On the form it read, *Grade 0. Communication. I have achieved in auditing the ability to communicate freely with anyone on any subject.*

There was a line for me to sign and date. I was ready to receive my certificate.

During the following days, Louis audited me on the rest of the Grades. Once I knew how the system worked, I passed each Grade quickly.

On Grade 1, by answering commands such as, "Invent a problem you could have with another," and, "Get the idea of solving a problem with that person," I finally realized that I could solve all my own problems.

I signed the Grade 1 attestation form that read, *Through processing I have made to vanish current problems in life and gained the ability to recognize the source of problems and make them vanish.*

The rest of the grades were similar. Grade 2, called Relief, had to do with guilt. At the end of that Grade, I realized I didn't have to feel guilty about anything in the past.

Grade 3 had to do with upsets with people, and Grade 4 had to do with fixed and destructive patterns of behavior. I learned that I often use my own imagined intellectual superiority to feel better than the people around me.

I posted my five signed and sealed certificates on the tiny space of wall above my mattress and gazed at them with intense satisfaction. I was halfway to Clear!

One day soon after that, Aileen called me into her office. "The LA Org is on a crash program to get new people into the building and on course." She peered at me over her glasses. "I've been ordered to send a staff person over there on a temporary basis to work in Div 6. You're the only one I have who's available to go."

I knew that Division 6 had to do with getting new people into Scientology. All Scientology centers at the time were set up on the same basis—six divisions, each containing three subdivisions.

Division 1, called HCO, Hubbard Communications Office, was divided into three subsections that were in charge of the training of staff, communications, and Ethics.

Division 2, called Dissem, for Dissemination, controlled the distribution of promo, supplying books and other publications, and the routine flooding of mail to all possible candidates for Org services.

Division 3, Organization, contained the branches in charge of income, disbursements, and property.

Division 4, Tech, for Technical, contained three departments that served to register incoming preclears and deliver training and auditing to the public.

Division 5, Qualifications, contained the department of Examinations (the Examiner), the department of Review (for people who were having problems in auditing or training), and the department of Certificates and Awards.

Division 6, Distribution, handled public activities, training of FSMs, or Field Staff Members, and the collection of Success Stories. That was the division to which I was assigned.

I walked over to the Org and reported to the Distribution Secretary, a tall, lean, very good-looking man named Jim. He introduced me to his assistant, a bubbly, short, blonde named Martha. She was in charge of giving all the lectures, which she was particularly qualified to do because she spoke fluent Spanish. She would be in charge of my training.

First, I had to take a short course that would teach me to effectively disseminate Scientology. Soon I found myself in a classroom with a study pack in my hands. Again, I studied the sage words of Hubbard.

> Scientology is a science of knowing how to know answers. It is an organized system of Axioms and Processes that resolve the problems of existence.
>
> This science is formed in the tradition of 10,000 years of religious philosophy and considers itself a culmination of the searches that began with the Veda, the

> Tao, Buddhism, Christianity, and other religions. Scientology is a Gnostic faith in that it knows it knows.

Gnostic? I wondered, looking up the word in the New World Dictionary. The definition seemed a bit circular—*Gnostic. Of the Gnostics or Gnosticism.*

I looked at the next definition.

> Gnosticism. A system of belief combining ideas derived from Greek philosophy, Oriental mysticism, and ultimately, Christianity, and stressing salvation through gnosis.

All right, I thought. *What's gnosis?* I looked it up.

> Gnosis. Positive, intuitive knowledge in spiritual matters, such as the Gnostics claimed to have.

I need an encyclopedia! I thought in exasperation.

Scientology didn't have encyclopedias, only dictionaries. I made a mental note to ask Antonio later and continued reading.

> Scientology can demonstrate that it can attain the goals set for men by Christ, which are: Wisdom, Good Health, and Immortality.

On lecturing to the public, Hubbard taught:

> In addressing the general public at large, a Scientologist has a responsibility to give to the public...information acceptable to them, which can be understood by them,

and which will send them away with the impression that the Scientologist who addressed them knew definitely what he was talking about and that Scientology is an unconfused, clear-cut subject.

A Scientologist, when addressing public groups, would never under any circumstances confuse his communication line by engaging in a debate from the floor with anyone who would care to heckle him. By simply ignoring such people, one continues to talk to the bulk of the people who are very interested. When anyone causes an unseemly upset, it's rarely difficult to have the person removed from the group. In other words, either ignore him or remove him. Don't engage in a debate with him.

The most important thing I learned in the new class was how to get people into Scientology. It was simple. We used a four-step drill devised by Hubbard called the Dissemination Drill.

> CONTACT the individual. This is plain and simple. It just means making a personal contact with someone, whether you approach them or they approach you.
> HANDLE. Handle is to handle any attacks, antagonism, challenge, or hostility that the individual might express toward you and/or Scientology.
> SALVAGE. Definition of salvage: "to save from ruin." Before you can save someone

from ruin, you must find out what their own personal ruin is.

BRING TO UNDERSTANDING. Once the person is aware of the ruin, you bring about an understanding that Scientology can handle the condition found in Step 3.

The Supervisor assigned me to "twin" on this course with Charlie, a tall, middle-aged man with curly, dark hair.

"I don't understand how to do this drill," I complained to Charlie.

"OK. Watch. It's simple. I'll show you how to do it. Let's set up the situation. I'll be a Scientologist. Let's say we're both on an airplane together, and you are sitting next to me. My object is to get you interested in Scientology and ready to sign up for a course. Ready?"

I nodded.

He came over, pulled up a chair beside me, and pretended to read a book.

I looked at him. He looked up and smiled.

"Hi, I'm Charlie. I noticed you were studying. You must be a student." He continued smiling.

"Yeah. I'm in college. I have a big psychology exam tomorrow." I looked back at my imaginary book, trying to ignore him.

"Oh, really? Are you interested in people?" He turned toward me.

"Yeah, I guess so. I like to try to understand why people act the way they do."

"That's very interesting. What did you say your name was?"

"I didn't. It's Margery. I'm on my way to Los Angeles."

"Say, if you're interested in people, you might be interested in the book I'm reading. It's about Scientology." He turned the book over, so I could see the cover.

"What's Scientology? I never heard of it."

"It's a wonderful new science about people, similar to psychology but actually more advanced. You'd probably really like it. They have a new type of counseling, called auditing. By learning to be an auditor, you can really help people with their problems."

"Are you sure it's not some kind of weird cult?" I asked suspiciously.

"Oh, no. It's a science. Everything in it has been fully and scientifically validated. Let me ask you a question. Did you ever have a problem? I mean, something you just couldn't seem to find an answer to?"

"Sure. Everyone has problems. You can't be alive and not have a problem," I replied noncommittally.

"Well, just give me an example of something in your life that has been a real problem to you."

"I guess just talking to people. I've always had trouble just talking. Lots of times I can't think of the right thing to say, especially to guys."

"What if I told you that there was a course you could take that would enable you to be able to talk to any person freely on any subject? Money back guaranteed."

"You're kidding." I looked at him, then I started laughing. "OK. You got me. That was too easy. Let's do it again, and this time, I'll be tougher."

"Fine."

We repeated the drill, but that time, I was antagonistic.

"Oh, yeah. I've heard about Scientology. They're just a bunch of kooks. I read all about it in *Time*. They're crazies." I waved my hand in disgust.

"Well," Charlie began in a diplomatic, soothing tone, "have you ever really talked to someone who was in Scientology?"

"No, I have to admit I haven't."

"Do you think you can believe everything you read in magazines and newspapers?"

"No. I guess you have a point there."

"I'm a Scientologist, and I'd just like to tell you a little about my experiences in Scientology. Maybe, I can prove to you that not every Scientologist is a flake."

"Well, all right," I said reluctantly.

Charlie launched into a convincing testimonial.

"You're really good at this," I said admiringly.

"You will be, too, with a few days of drilling. Now it's your turn."

For the rest of the day, Charlie drilled me until I knew the four steps of the dissemination drill cold. During the following days, I twinned up with various people on the course until I was proficient in locating the person's ruin and telling them about Scientology.

"Now you're ready to do it for real," the Supervisor said, signing off my check sheet and sending me back to Martha and Jim.

I was given the job of going out on the street near the Org and procuring people to come into the building for a beginning lecture on Scientology.

"Here's the system," Martha confided. "You just get the bodies in the shop. Then it's up to Jim and me to get them signed up for a course."

"How do you do that?" I asked.

"Easy. First, I give them a short lecture, then I send them to Jim, who signs them up for a course or to buy a book."

She sent me out to round up people for the three-o'clock lecture.

I wandered around the center. There was no one in sight. Finally, I walked to Alvarado Street, but there were just a few drunks walking or staggering along the street in the simmering afternoon heat, so I returned to the Org.

"Martha, there's no one to bring in, just a few drunks. How am I supposed to bring anyone in, in this area? This isn't exactly Beverly Hills."

"Flunk for having considerations. Just go out and bring in some people. That's an order."

"You mean even drunks?"

"I mean anyone. We need bodies in the shop. We need stats. What makes you think that an alcoholic doesn't need what we have to offer? Just go and bring back some people."

I walked obediently back onto the street and saw an elderly couple walking slowly toward me.

"Hi," I said. "I'd like to invite you to a lecture on Scientology. It's free."

They replied in Spanish, and I realized they didn't speak English. I motioned them to follow me. If I could just get them to Martha, she could take over. I walked with them toward the Org, gesturing wildly toward the building. Taking them by the arm, I led them up the steps.

"Martha, I don't speak Spanish," I said quickly. "Here." I brought over my two bewildered captives.

Martha smiled and spoke in fluent Spanish, leading them toward the lecture room. "Now go get some more," she commanded.

I walked out and wandered around for a while in the area. Soon, I found a young man sitting on the grass near the park.

"Would you like to come to a free lecture?" I asked.

He stared at me with glazed eyes. It was clear what his ruin was. His arms were covered with needle marks, and he didn't seem able to speak.

I gestured and told him to come with me. Eventually, he managed to stand and lurch in my direction. I assumed he hoped I would offer him drugs or worse.

I led him back to the center. Martha took him to a seat in the front row. I saw the Spanish couple seated at Jim's desk, while he asked them for money.

"Jim, they don't speak English," I said softly.

"I know that." He waved me away. He was almost yelling at the couple, telling them that he needed some money, even just a quarter, and they had to sign the form on his desk. I watched as eventually, in confusion, they finally understood he wanted money, and they gave him a quarter. Then they signed the form and left.

"What good does it do when they didn't understand what they were doing?" I asked Jim. "I don't think they'll come back."

"It doesn't matter." He looked at me emphatically. "As long as they give me some money, I can count it as a stat. It's up to the Registrar to contact them and get them in on course."

Martha arrived leading the drug addict and sat him down beside Jim. The man looked completely dazed. I watched in wonder, as Jim managed to extract a few pennies from him and got him to sign a very wobbly signature on the registration form.

For the rest of the week, I continued bringing bodies in. Sometimes, I was given a stack of paperback Dianetics books to take out to the street to sell for five dollars each. At the end of the day, when I had made hardly any sales, I was reduced to begging people to buy my books. To my surprise, some did.

When 2:00 on Thursday came, we turned in our stats to HCO. It looked as if we had a good week, yet only two people had been registered for a course.

As weeks passed, I worked desperately to get more people into the Org. I was becoming more and more exhausted and less and less able to convince people to come with me for the free lecture. The truth was, I didn't want to go back myself. What bothered me was that I had seen Jim and Martha inflate the statistics they reported every week. I counted the number of people I brought back to the center, yet their stats were consistently 100% above the number I brought in. In the strict order of things done in Scientology, that was illegal. I knew what I had to do.

I wrote up a Knowledge Report and sent it with my stats the following Thursday to the Sea Org headquarters at Saint Hill, where each week the statistics for all organizations worldwide were tabulated and analyzed. I knew my report would cause what's known in Scientology as a "flap," or trouble. I was right.

One day I was summoned into the office of the Ethics Officer at the Org. Unlike the Ethics Officer at Celebrity Center, he wasn't in uniform. He was a young man in his twenties who wore the nondescript clothes of a longtime staff member, a white shirt and faded, worn, dark pants.

"Did you write this?" He held a copy of the report I'd mailed out the previous week.

"Yes. Publics is sending in false stats every week."

"Why didn't you come to see me before you sent this to Worldwide?" he demanded angrily. "Do you realize that you managed to get me in a lot of trouble?"

"I didn't mean to," I apologized. "I just thought, if it concerned the stats, it had to go to the people who collect the stats."

"You've caused a serious flap for the Org, when it was something that could very easily have been handled internally. A two-man mission will come here tomorrow from the ship to investigate. I don't have to tell you what that means. Some heads will roll, thanks to you." He slammed his fist down on the table.

Fear crept up my spine.

"You're hereby declared to be in a condition of Enemy to this organization," he said menacingly. "Until this whole thing is resolved, you'll be working with Estates and sleeping here in the Org."

He came over to me with a piece of gray rag in his hand. I knew only too well what it was for. He tied the rag around my upper arm.

"I'm instructing Estates to give you the hardest labor they can find while you work yourself out of your condition," he said darkly.

"What do I have to do?" I felt like crying. I knew the humiliation I'd feel when I walked out of his office with the dreaded rag tied to my arm. It meant, among other things, that no one was allowed to speak to me.

"Look it up." He handed me the Ethics book.

I located the paragraph entitled *Condition of Enemy*.

> When a person is an avowed and knowing enemy of an individual, a group, project, or

organization, a Condition of Enemy exists.

The formula for the Condition of Enemy is just one step: FIND OUT WHO YOU REALLY ARE.

"How am I supposed to do that?" I asked, feeling slightly defiant.

"That's your problem," he said coldly. "You'll just have to figure it out." He opened the door, obviously wanting me to leave.

I left the room, not knowing where to go, and slowly walked up to the Receptionist in the lobby. "Where is Estates?"

When she saw the rag, a look of fear crossed her face. Without speaking, she motioned me to follow. I realized she wasn't allowed to speak to me even to give me directions.

We walked to the north side of the building, and she pointed toward a low white shed behind the annex. I turned to thank her, but she had already walked back to the Org.

I located the Estates I/C (In Charge), a very old man in a blue work suit.

"Got yourself in trouble, eh?" Apparently, he didn't know the rule about not talking.

"Yeah, I guess." I was glad I could talk to someone. "What do I have to do?"

"You'll be doing some cleaning." He had a slight Scottish accent. He handed me a giant bucket and some rags. "Take these. You might as well start by washing the latrines. Here's some soap." He handed me a bottle of golden liquid. "You just need a little bit in each bucket of water. Go easy, or it'll eat up your hands."

I walked slowly back to the Org. Several people stared, noticing the symbol of humiliation on my arm.

Alone in the mercifully deserted women's bathroom, I realized the full impact of my situation. *I've let everyone down,* I thought miserably, as my tears mixed with the soapy water on the floor. *What will Aileen think when she finds out? What will Antonio think?*

I thought of my friends at the center, and I knew I had betrayed them all. Worst of all, I disappointed the one person I respected above all others in the world and universe.

"Ron. Dad. I disappointed you again." As I cried, old pain from the past fused with pain from the present.

My world fell into a thousand shattered pieces around me, as I sat on the dirty tiled bathroom floor. I felt more completely alone in that moment than I ever felt before or since Scientology. I came face-to-face with the terror and finality of my own wretched inadequacy as a human being.

The formula is right after all, I thought. *Find out who you really are.*

I knew the answer. *I'm a Scientologist. Nothing else matters. I'll never fail my group again.*

CHAPTER ELEVEN

Welcome to the RPF

I fished the rag out of the dirty, gray water in the pail then squeezed it to drip water on the filthy tiles. Taking the brush I'd been given by Gus, the old man in charge of Estates, I scrubbed the last section of tile.

Before I began, the floor appeared dirty gray, but as I cleaned, an intricate pattern of blue and white tiles in an Indian design emerged from the filth. *How long has it been since they cleaned this bathroom?* I wondered, looking at my finished work in satisfaction. *I'll feel this tomorrow,* I thought ruefully. That was the sixth bathroom I cleaned since beginning my penance several hours earlier. It was dark outside.

I undid the window latches and forced it halfway open. A cool evening breeze floated into the room. I wiped a trickle of sweat from my forehead with my arm and looked with dismay at my hands. *He wasn't kidding about the soap,* I thought, trying to dry the raw skin on my slacks.

I looked at the courtyard below, where clusters of students gathered, and listened to the sounds of laughter and conversation drifting up to the window. *It must be nine o'clock. Break time.* I longed to be part of the happy scene below. *Instead, here I am, the Cinderella of Scientology.*

I closed the window and gathered my cleaning supplies before heading back to Estates. I desperately wanted a shower. A hot shower, with or without roaches, suddenly seemed an incredible luxury, one I previously took for granted.

Gus saw me coming. "Over here."

He stood near the annex door.

"Come help me move these mattresses." He motioned me to follow.

Behind the annex was a large shed in ramshackle condition, looking as if it might collapse at any moment. I followed Gus inside and waited until my eyes adjusted to the dim light from a street lamp coming through a small window at the far end of the room. Stacks of what looked like thin mattresses were piled against the wall.

Gus switched on a small lamp in the corner. "Here. Give me a hand with these." He pulled the top mat from the pile. "Just put them on the floor about six inches apart. I guess this is where you'll be sleeping tonight—with the rest of the RPFers."

"RPFers?"

"Yeah, the rest of the folks in the RPF, the Rehabilitation Project Force. Didn't you know that's what you were in?"

"I never heard of it before. What's the Rehabilitation Project Force?"

"It's a new idea. I guess it came from Hubbard. I hear it started on the ship. It's for people who get themselves into trouble in the Org if they mess up or if their stats are too low. Quite a few people have come through here in the past month or so. You probably won't be here long." He regarded me optimistically. "Most folks don't stay here very long."

"So what do people do who are in the RPF?" I asked, almost too tired to care.

"Well, work, mostly." Gus put the last mat into place. "There. All set for the night."

I listened as he continued talking about the RPF.

"We take care of the property, painting, cleaning, things like that. I'm glad to have the help, believe me. Before the RPF, I had to manage everything myself. Right now, most of the men are working to renovate the Cedars Complex down on Berendo."

I heard about the huge complex of buildings that Scientology just bought for $5 million in cash. It was a labyrinthine complex that had previously been a hospital. According to rumor, it was to be the future home of Scientology in Los Angeles.

"They should be back before too long," Gus continued. "Then you'll be eating your dinner."

"Isn't it kind of late for dinner?"

"Yeah. In the beginning, I tried to do something about that, but I was told not to interfere. I tried to change a lot of things around here, but I was politely told to butt out and keep my ideas to myself. Around here," he lamented, "it doesn't pay to argue."

"So why do you stay? If you're unhappy, why stay?"

He considered his answer for several minutes. "I guess, because I believe in the Old Man. Hubbard. I was with him from the beginning, more than twenty years ago. Left my family and everything. I thought we were going to change the world. Turn it upside down." He looked at me sadly.

"I can't say it was a mistake, exactly. It just didn't turn out like I thought. Anyway, where would I go? I don't know where my family is. I plan to stick it out. One of these days, I'll probably drop the old body. It won't matter anymore."

We were silent awhile. I thought over what he said. I wanted to say something wise or comforting, but I couldn't think of anything. His life was a tragedy, but to feel sympathy was wrong, according to Hubbard—sympathy was an emotion very low on the Tone Scale. Hubbard's chart of the emotions was arranged in a hierarchy from Serenity of Beingness (+40.0) to Total Failure (-40.0).

A knock on the door interrupted the uncomfortable silence. The door opened, and twelve unbelievably dirty men, some looking very young, filtered into the room. All wore the same dark-blue work suit that Gus wore.

"I guess I'll be going over and getting your food," Gus said, sounding relieved to have something to do to distract him from painful memories. He walked out the door toward the Org.

"Welcome to the RPF." One of the older men looked at me curiously. "So what did you do to earn yourself a place in the RPF? Mess up a PC?"

"Not exactly," I said regretfully. "More like making the mistake of minding someone else's business. I stuck my nose in where it didn't belong. I wrote up a Knowledge Report that got some people in trouble, including Ethics."

"I guess you'll be here for a while." He chuckled. "Might as well make the best of it."

"There's no such thing as the best of it," grumbled the youngest of the group, who was barely a teenager. "This place is the pits. If I had any money, I'd be on the first bus out of here."

Some of the others grunted their agreement.

"Can't you leave?" I asked. "I mean, if you really want to? Who would stop you?"

"And go where?" The boy looked up at me. "With no money, where am I going to go?"

"Where's your family? Your parents? Don't you have a family to go back to?"

"No. They're all in Scientology on the ship. My grandparents are dead. There's nowhere for me to go." He punched his fist into the palm of his hand. "I'm stuck here for a billion years," he said sarcastically. "Scientology is a bunch of crap—the whole thing." He looked at me bitterly. "Hubbard's nothing but a con artist. This whole thing is nothing but a money-making racket." He hit the wall with his fist.

"Come on, Joey," another boy said. "We told you, if you keep talking like that, you'll never get out of here. They're just going to keep you in the RPF forever."

"I don't care. That's what I think. Nothing they do to me is going to make me change my mind. I can't believe my parents fell for this crap. Everything was fine before they got into Scientology. We had a house, car, everything. Now, nothing. They sold everything and gave all the money to Ron." He said the name sarcastically.

I was shocked by his heresies. "Haven't you had auditing?"

"No. I don't believe in it. I'm not going to waste my time. Yeah, if I go along with the program, I can get out of the RPF. Big deal. What for? I just don't agree with any of it. I'll stick it out here. I'll stay in the RPF for a billion years. I don't care, anyway." He rubbed his sore knuckles.

Nobody said a word. The sound of footsteps outside the door interrupted the silence. Gus came in carrying two pails in a box containing plates and spoons. I looked in the pails, but I couldn't identify the contents.

"Beans and rice." Gus answered my unspoken question. "Better get used to it. In the RPF, you'll be having it a lot."

I took a plate along with the others and spooned some of the unappetizing mixture onto my plate. "What's in the other bucket?"

"Bread crusts," Joey volunteered. "Help yourself."

I reached into the pail and pulled out a crust of bread. One side of the bread had a bite-sized indentation. "What in the world?" I stared in disbelief.

"You guessed it." Joey laughed despite himself at my chagrin. "Sometimes, we get scraps of bread left over from other people's plates."

Disgusted, I tossed the crust back into the pail. My appetite was gone. I ate a few spoonfuls of the rice-and-beans mixture and threw the rest into the trash.

Now what? I wondered, looking around. As the others finished eating, they lay on the mats.

"Don't we get a shower?" I asked the man who spoke to me first. "I'm filthy. I can't sleep like this."

"We get showers only every other day. We had them yesterday. We don't get one again until tomorrow night." He switched off the lamp.

I was too exhausted to argue. I lay on one of the mats. It was completely dark in the room except for the dim light from the street. I wanted to think, but I was just too tired. I finally fell into a fitful sleep, dreaming that I was on a large ship on an angry, rolling sea. I was on a never-ending voyage into unreality, on a ship that threatened to capsize at any moment, spilling us all into the infinite, anonymous water.

"Wake up." Someone shook me. "Come on, or you'll miss breakfast."

I opened my eyes. The room was dark.

"Come on. Hurry."

In confusion, I stumbled to my feet and followed the one who woke me. Outside, I looked up at the sky, which was beginning to show the first hopeful rays of the morning sun.

"What time is it?" I asked groggily, rubbing my eyes with grimy fists.

"Six-thirty." It was one of the men I met the previous night.

I followed him sleepily to the back door of the Org. We walked back into a tiny kitchen. I was handed a plate of toast, bacon, and something that looked vaguely like oatmeal. I tasted it. It was cold and tasteless.

"You'll want to eat it," a voice behind me advised.

I turned and saw the older man from the previous night. "I'm sorry. I didn't introduce myself last night." I held out my hand. "I was too exhausted to think. I'm Margery."

"Larry." He shook my hand and led me to the steps outside the back door. The others were there, sitting and eating the unsavory meal.

"You have to learn to eat the food," Larry said, swallowing oatmeal. "Otherwise, you'll get weak. Just visualize something you really like and swallow fast. After a while, you'll be hungry enough that anything will taste good to you."

I took a bite of the oatmeal and tried to swallow it quickly. I thought of the delicious hot cereal my mother made with butter and maple syrup, but it didn't help.

By seven o'clock, the sun was emerging. Rays of pink and orange thrust into the grayness above us. A surge of optimism swelled within me, as sleepiness gave way to the energy of a new day. Despite sore muscles from the previous day's work, I was ready to live again.

Scientology, you can't break me, I thought. *I'm a survivor. I can overcome this temporary setback. I'll prove that I can be a valuable member of the group.*

A truck arrived to transport the men to the Cedars Complex, where they'd be working.

"What about me?" I asked the driver. "I don't know if I'm supposed to go."

"I think you're supposed to help the Registrars," he replied. "Go to the second floor and try the third door on your right. I think they're expecting you."

I followed his directions and found a girl about my own age with thick, dark hair, sitting at a desk surrounded by tall stacks of manila folders.

"Oh, good," she said, as I entered. "Are you Margery?"

I nodded.

"I'm Audrey. I'm so glad you're here. We're way behind on our stats."

She pulled up a chair to a small desk across from hers, also piled with folders, and cleared a small space amid the jungle of paperwork.

"All you have to do is take a folder," she began. "Go through it quickly and look at the recent correspondence. Then write a short letter to the person urging them to come in for the next service. That's all there is to it. Our quota for Normal Operation (an Ethics condition) is twenty letters an hour. Here's some paper and pens. Envelopes are in that box." She brought me a handful of envelopes.

I opened one of the folders and found a stack of unanswered letters inside. Apparently, the person had ignored all of them.

"Audrey?"

She looked up from her work.

"This person has been sent over twenty letters and hasn't answered any of them." I showed her the folder.

"That doesn't matter. We just keep on writing. You'd be surprised. Sometimes, we'll write fifty letters to a person without an answer, and after the fiftieth letter, suddenly we get a response. Anyway, each letter you write counts as a stat, and that's all that really matters." She quickly returned to writing.

I began writing.

Dear Stephanie,

I hope you'll come in soon for your free personality test. Did you enjoy the Dianetics book?

I signed the letter and stuffed it into the envelope. It was easy enough.

Soon, I was in production. The room was totally quiet. Several hours passed. It was almost relaxing.

Suddenly, I heard someone yelling in the hall. A short, bent woman burst into the room. She had white hair, and her face was very red.

"Audrey, where are my things?" she cried hysterically. "All my things are missing from my room. What have they done with my things?"

The Ethics Officer appeared behind her. "Ruby," he said sternly, "you've been *declared* and are not to be on these premises. I told you, you weren't to come back into this house."

"But where are my things?" she wailed.

"Out there. Out in front. Now you must leave, or I'll have to call the police." He took her arm and led her, still crying hysterically, down the stairs.

Audrey walked to the front window, and I followed. There, on the pavement, were two large heavy-duty black trash bags stuffed with what appeared to be clothes and other personal items.

"Poor Ruby," Audrey said under her breath.

"What happened to her?"

Audrey sat on the ledge and cupped her hands over her eyes. "I feel so sorry for her," she said softly, looking up at me. "Ruby just got too old. She worked here for sixteen years, but lately, she started messing up. She lost folders and wrote letters that didn't make sense. She started talking funny, too. They finally held a Comm Ev on her. She was declared SP, and they decided to offload her."

"Offload?" I'd never heard the term and wondered what Ruby had done to be sent before a Committee of Evidence, the Scientology equivalent of a jury trial.

"Yes. That's when they send you away with orders that you aren't allowed to come back into Scientology. If a person becomes a problem to the Org, they're usually offloaded. Ethics just wants to get rid of them, but Ruby...." She didn't speak for a while, then she looked up. "Ruby didn't deserve this."

"Where will she go?" I looked out the door and saw Ruby struggling to lift one of the bags. "Why didn't they call her family or get her help?"

"How long have you been around?" she asked, her tone changing suddenly. "Don't you know that when you get old or sick, it's your own responsibility? That's what Hubbard says. We're all responsible for our own condition, no matter what happens. Nobody can be responsible for you except yourself. The same with Ruby. She has to be responsible for herself, and she will. She's a strong thetan." Audrey turned away from the window.

"Let's get back to work. The stats have been down since Ruby left, and we'll really have to work to get them back up again."

I sat at my desk, wanting to go down and help Ruby, but what could I do? Something about the situation bothered me, but, when I tried to think about it, I felt more confused.

"Ron knows best," I said. "The greatest good for the greatest number of dynamics. That's the rule we have to follow, or we'll never get the job done. There's no time to be sorry for someone like Ruby."

Just the same, I thought of her frequently for many days, remembering the fear in her eyes, which was that of a terrified animal.

We sat and silently wrote letters the rest of the day. I was given a decent lunch and dinner. I stayed at work until eleven o'clock that night, then walked back to the shack behind the annex. My fellow RPFers were already asleep. I wanted a shower, but I didn't want to wake anyone to ask where it was.

The following morning, we were again awakened in the misty dawn and ate a breakfast like the previous day. Larry was right. With hunger, it tasted better.

The driver arrived in his truck. "Climb aboard," he told me. "I have orders to take you with me to the Guardian's Office to help with some filing." He looked at a piece of paper in his hand. "Is your name Margery?"

"That's me." I got into the truck and glanced at myself in the rearview mirror. I grimaced. I looked terrible. My hair was matted, and smudges of dirt covered my face. My clothes were soiled and wrinkled. I was glad no one at the center could see me.

The Cedars was a short drive away. I followed the driver inside the building, and he led me to an elevator. Inside, he punched the button for the third floor. A sign near the buttons read, *Third Floor. Guardian's Office. Authorized Personnel Only.*

The door opened, and I looked around curiously. I didn't know much about the Guardian's Office, just what Hubbard told us, that they had the job of making the world safe for Scientology to expand into.

A receptionist sat at a desk blocking the long hallway.

"The RPF for filing," the driver said brusquely, then turned and caught the elevator just as the door closed.

"Have a seat." The receptionist eyed me with distaste. I took the seat farthest from the desk.

Minutes later, a woman in a navy-blue uniform came out and motioned me to follow her. She led me down the hall to a small room filled with filing cabinets.

"We've got a real backlog right now with our filing," she said, surveying the room. "Ethics has ordered you to help us out. Here's a pile to start with." She selected a stack of papers from a table on which hundreds of pieces of paper were piled precariously. "Find the person's folder and file this inside. Here's a punch. Punch holes and file it on the top-left side of the folder. The folders are in these cabinets in alphabetical order." Handing me a hole punch, she left the room.

A short time later, I was surprised to see the Ethics Officer in the doorway. He stood over me wordlessly for a moment, then asked coldly, "Have you started working your way out of your Condition?"

"You mean Enemy?"

He didn't reply.

"Yes, in fact, I have. I thought about it the night I was cleaning bathrooms. I know for sure now who I am and where I belong. I won't harm the group again," I said sincerely.

"Here's some paper." He handed me a sheet. "Write it up and submit it to me later today. Perhaps I can upgrade you to Doubt."

I was about to thank him, but he had already left the room. I took the sheet of paper and printed my name and the words *Condition of Enemy* at the top, then I underlined them before I began.

> I was in a Condition of Enemy, because I betrayed two members of my group. I got them and the Org into trouble by writing a Knowledge Report and sending it to World Wide instead of just going to see Ethics.
>
> I'll never again do anything to harm my group. I know now who I am. I'm a Scientologist. Scientology is my group, and I just want to be a good member of the group. I wish to be upgraded to a Condition of Doubt.

I printed my name below and then signed it. Folding the paper, I walked out to the receptionist. "How can I get this to the Ethics Officer?" I asked.

"Give it to me," she said, taking the paper from me. "I'll see that he gets it."

I walked back to my filing.

Later that afternoon, the receptionist walked back into my room. "Here." She handed me a folded piece of paper. "The Ethics Officer says you're to work out of Doubt."

"Do you have an Ethics book?"

She nodded and left. A few minutes later, she handed me a copy of the book, and I looked up the Doubt formula.

I was to evaluate the group to which I belonged as an Enemy (of Scientology) and also the group of Scientology.

> Join or remain in the one which progresses toward the greatest good for the greatest number of dynamics and announce the fact publicly to both sides.
>
> Do everything possible to improve the actions and statistics of the person, group, project, or organization one has remained in or joined.
>
> Suffer on up through the conditions of the group one has remained in if wavering from it has lowered one's status.

I opened the blank sheet I'd been given and wrote my name at the top and the words *Condition of Doubt*.

> Until I did this formula, I didn't realize how important the group of Scientology was to me. Now I know for sure that Scientology is my group. It's the group that's doing the most for the planet. I'll never betray my group again. From now on, I only want to do what I can to help my group, because to help the group is to help the planet. I'm no longer in Doubt.

I sent it back to the Ethics Officer.

I returned to the Org to eat dinner that evening. Thankfully, Gus showed me where the shower was, and I enjoyed the luxury of a hot shower. Never again would I take a shower for granted.

I returned to the annex, shaking out my hair to dry in the warm evening air. Gus met me at the door.

"You're to report back to the GO," he announced. "He said to tell you to report at once as soon as you got back. I can give you a ride there."

"Thanks. Do you know what it's about?"

"No," he said, adding under his breath, "and I don't want to know."

"Why? What could it be?"

"You'll find out soon enough."

We climbed into his truck.

I walked to the reception desk and found a different woman there. She led me back to the small room where I'd been filing.

"You've been upgraded to Liability," she said, her face an expressionless mask. "Do you know the formula?"

"I'd have to look at the book," I confessed.

The Ethics book I'd used earlier was still on my desk. She nodded, and I quickly turned to the appropriate page.

> Condition of Liability
>
> Decide who are one's friends.
>
> Deliver an effective blow to the enemies of the group one has been pretending to be part of despite personal danger.
>
> Make up the damage one has done by personal contribution far beyond the ordinary demands of a group member.
>
> Apply for reentry to the group by asking the permission of each member of it to rejoin and rejoining only by majority permission.

"OK." I looked at the uniformed woman. "I know who my friends are. Scientologists are my friends. Scientologists in good standing. Scientology is my group. How can I deliver an effective blow to the enemies of the group?"

"Are you willing to take that step even if it means some danger to yourself?" Her eyes were intense as she asked.

"Sure. How could I be in danger?"

"Wait here." She walked out.

Several minutes later, she reappeared in the doorway with a tall, blond man wearing a dark Sea Org uniform. He didn't waste time on preliminaries or introductions. I never learned his name.

"We have a job for you," he said abruptly, "that will satisfy your Liability Formula.

"A few blocks from here is a psychiatrist's office. This man has been causing us some problems with the American Psychiatric Association. It's not important for you to know what those problems are." He stopped to clear his throat.

"We want you to get into his office. Pretend to be a patient or whatever you like. Somewhere on his bookshelf should be a directory of all the psychiatrists in the United States. We need that directory and anything else you can bring us—financial information, the names of his clients, anything. Can you handle it?"

I took a deep breath and looked at the formula again. Hubbard said psychiatry was evil, a holdover from nineteenth century German behavioral therapy. According to Hubbard, psychiatrists were our chief enemies on the planet. They used barbaric methods to treat people with psychiatric problems, including lobotomies and electroshock treatment. It was up to Scientology to end such barbaric practices, and I could help.

"OK." I looked at him. "Where's the office? You don't care how I get in?"

"No. We don't care how you do it. We just want those records. I probably don't have to tell you that if there's any trouble, under no circumstances can you implicate the Org or Scientology. Do you understand?"

"Yeah, I understand. I won't get caught. You'll see." I felt confident I could do the job.

He handed me a slip of paper with the address. "You'll need some fresh clothes." He appraised my wrinkled apparel before saluting the receptionist and walking out.

Wow, I thought. *I don't believe this. I get to be a spy!* The knowledge that I was about to perform an illegal act was offset by the thought that I'd be doing a great service for my group. It would also get me out of Liability. I couldn't wait to begin.

I walked back to the deserted house on Beacon Street. *At least tonight I can sleep in my own bed,* I thought. Selecting slacks and my best blouse, I went into the kitchen to iron them.

Shortly afterward, I fell into a deep, dreamless sleep. When I awoke, the house was empty.

I went into the kitchen to find a clock. It was nine-thirty, which meant I'd really overslept. I took a quick shower and put on my clean clothes, then I rummaged through the kitchen for a grocery bag, which I folded and stuffed into my purse. I set out to find the address on the slip of paper.

Soon, I stood outside a low building with a sign over the door that read, *Habana Professional Building.* I quickly located the building directory in a glass case in the lobby.

I looked up the name I'd been given for the troublesome psychiatrist and found it listed in room 203. I climbed the stairs to the second floor and opened the door to the waiting room.

A secretary behind a glass window looked at me pleasantly. "May I help you?"

"Yes. I'd like to make an appointment with the doctor. A friend referred me to him. Is he here?"

"No, but I expect him back around one o'clock this afternoon." She opened a small black book on her desk. "How about four o'clock this Thursday?"

"I'm afraid it's a bit of an emergency," I said, trying to sound desperate. "Does he have anything sooner?"

"Well, he might have a cancellation at one o'clock today. Would you like to return at noon?"

"Would you mind if I waited here?" I pleaded. "I live quite a way from here. There isn't time for me to go home and return. I'll just sit here and read."

"All right," she said reluctantly. "Make yourself comfortable. I should know about the cancellation in about an hour." She smiled and returned to her work.

I took a chair in the waiting room and pretended to read a recent issue of *Time*. From the corner of my eye, I watched everything that happened behind the glass window.

An hour later, the receptionist called out, "You're in luck. The other patient just cancelled. The doctor will see you at one o'clock."

She stood and came into the waiting room with her purse. "I'm going out for a quick lunch. I'll be back in a few minutes. If you need anything, the bookkeeper is in the back room."

That was what I'd been waiting for. The moment she left, I quietly opened the door to the receptionist's area and looked at the books on her desk. There wasn't much except the doctor's appointment book.

It would be safer to take that on the way out, I thought, looking toward the back, where I heard the bookkeeper talking on the phone.

I noiselessly opened the door to the doctor's office. If I were caught, I would say I was looking for something interesting to read.

Inside were many bookshelves. I scanned the titles until I found one labeled *APA Directory*. I pulled it off the shelf and opened it. *Perfect.* There were rows and rows of names and addresses.

Checking the other books on the shelf, I saw nothing interesting, just old copies of journals bound into notebooks.

I stealthily opened the door and listened. The voice in the back room was still talking to someone on the phone. I quietly closed the door and crept to the secretary's desk to snap up the appointment book and place the books in the bag I had brought.

I walked nonchalantly out of the building and started down the street. One block away, I began running.

That was too easy, I thought triumphantly. *It was way too easy.* My heart pounded.

I didn't bother returning to the house. Instead, I went to the Cedars Complex and found the secretary on the second floor.

"It worked," I gasped, out of breath from running. "I got everything you wanted. Well, almost everything. I couldn't find any financial records." I handed her the two books.

She looked through them. "Wait here." She pointed to a chair beside her desk.

Several minutes later, the man in the Sea Org uniform came to the lobby. "I'll let the Ethics Officer know you performed this errand satisfactorily." He held up the two books. "I'm impressed by the speed with which you carried out this mission. As Ron says, 'Speed of particle flow equals power.' You may return to the Org and report to Ethics. I don't want you to mention this to anyone—ever. Do you understand?"

"Perfectly." I felt like saluting and almost glowed under the praise he gave me.

I began the long walk back to the Org.

"Are you ready to complete the formula?" the Ethics Officer asked without referring to the events earlier that day.

"I have to make up the damage by extraordinary personal contribution," I quoted. "How can I do that?"

"Normally, we'd have you do work for seventy-two hours to get out of Liability, but since you apparently did an excellent job for the Guardian's Office, I'll reduce that to forty-eight hours," he said magnanimously.

He took me down to the Registrar's Office.

"Excuse me," he said to Audrey, who sat at her desk writing letters. He pointed to me and added, "She has to do forty-eight hours of amends. Please arrange for someone to supervise her on the night shift." He left.

Audrey smiled and said softly, "Don't worry. It won't be as bad as you think."

I sat down and took a pile of folders.

For the next two days and two nights, I wrote letters. I was too excited about my successful spy caper to sleep much the first night. To Audrey's credit, when I dozed off during the second day, she ignored it unless she heard someone approaching the office, in which case she called my name to rouse me from my sleep.

During the second night, I was too sleepy to remember much. The night watchman, who luckily was a kind, older man, came by every half hour to make sure I was busy writing. I got so I could doze off just as he left the room and awaken a short time later. He caught me napping a couple of times, but he just woke me and left chuckling.

Finally, I was allowed to return to the Org to sleep. I collapsed on a mat on the annex floor and slept from noon that day until the following morning.

Walking back to the Org that day, I thought of Hubbard's words in the Ethics book.

> All that Ethics is for—the totality of the reason for its existence and operation—is simply that additional tool necessary to make it possible to apply the technology of Scientology.
>
> We're factually here only helping people help themselves to better their condition and the conditions of life. That's our total action.
>
> As that additional tool for making it all possible, the Ethics system of Scientology is tremendously successful.

"I guess it is." I laughed. "I never want to get into a lower condition again. From now on, I'll keep my ethics in!"

CHAPTER TWELVE

Have You Ever Enslaved a Population?

> I'm a Scientologist. I know now that my true friends are other Scientologists in good standing. I'll never harm my group again. I want to do only those things that will contribute to the survival of my group, and, therefore, to the survival of the planet. I've delivered a blow to the enemies of the group and performed forty-eight hours of amends. I hereby petition to rejoin staff at the LA Org.

For two days, I carried my petition from person to person at the Org, begging each one to allow me to rejoin the group. Finally, I had the required signatures and ran upstairs to the Ethics officer.

"Here you are, Sir," I said. "I got everyone to sign."

He took the clipboard from me and glanced through the signatures. "Very well done. I hope you've learned something from this."

"Yes, Sir, I have," I said eagerly. "Mostly I learned something about being a part of a group, how you have to work with people, not against them. From now on, I want to stay out of trouble—with Ethics, I mean. I'd rather not have to go through all this again."

"Hmmm." He opened a desk drawer and took out a manila folder. To my surprise, it had my name on it followed by the words, *Ethics File.*

"I see here that this is your first major Ethics offense," he observed, flipping through the file's contents. "Let's hope it's the last. All right. You may return to your post."

"Great!" I bounded up from my chair and looked back at him. "Thank you, Sir." I moved toward the door.

"Aren't you forgetting something?" He pointed at my arm.

"Oh. I almost forgot. I guess I was getting used to it." I walked over and held out my arm, as he untied the unsightly rag. "I'm glad to be rid of that."

For the next several months, I worked in the Public Division, selling books on the street or bringing people in for the free lecture or free personality test. The personality test, I learned, was just another way of finding someone's ruin. After we graded the test, we pointed out the lowest score to the person and had him agree he needed help in that area. Then we sold him a course or some auditing to remedy the deficit. It always worked.

I initiated a program to take the paperback *Dianetics* book to the campuses of UCLA and USC to sell to students. With continued drilling on the Dissem Formula, it was easy to get students signed up for the Communication Course. We even started a Scientology group on campus and had regular meetings.

I soon learned to spot the students who made the best targets—the ones who were alone and seemed unhappy. They were the easiest to recruit into Scientology, because they were hungry for friendship and affiliation.

They decided I'd remain on staff at the Org instead of Celebrity Center, because the Org more desperately needed help. Since the Org and the center were close to each other, I could always visit the center on my breaks.

Because of my success with the psychiatrist's office, I was occasionally summoned back to the GO, Guardian's Office, to help on special projects. Many were enjoyable, especially the ones designed to improve the public image of Scientology in Los Angeles. We had a big Easter egg hunt for local children on the Org's lawn. Each GO project always had a unique, significant name. The Easter egg hunt was known to us as Operation Bunny Hop.

Operation Clean Sweep was a Saturday all-hands project to clean up the trash in Alvarado Park. In Operation Granny, teams of Scientology ministers brought cheer to the elderly in nearby nursing homes. A project to get Scientologists into the schools to give lectures against drug abuse was called Operation Chalk Dust.

The point of those projects wasn't so much to clean up the park, improve the lives of the elderly, or to educate children about drugs as it was to improve the image of Scientology, and, whenever possible, bring new people into the organization. That was the true agenda behind any apparent intent of a Scientologist—get new people to join and Clear the planet.

In the 1970s, Scientology, and the Guardian's Office in particular, had two major problems—Paulette Cooper and Michael Meisner.

In 1971, Paulette Cooper wrote a book critical of Scientology called *The Scandal of Scientology.* Repeated attempts to silence her, including attempts to frame her by getting her fingerprints on a piece of paper that was later used to send a death threat to Henry Kissinger, and by phoning the Arab consulate in New York and saying Cooper was talking about bombing them, met with minimal success. A more permanent solution was needed.

Michael Meisner was involved in a complicated Scientology plot in the mid-70s to illegally photocopy and steal thousands of government documents from FBI and IRS offices in Washington, DC. The FBI caught him, and, although he was back in Scientology custody, he threatened to turn state's evidence and incriminate the organization in a host of related criminal actions.

As a GO volunteer, I was given the sensitive task of going through all of Michael Meisner's supposedly confidential preclear and Ethics folders and locating anything we could use to blackmail him. I was told to be particularly alert for information regarding sexual deviance or criminal behavior. I had to circle anything I found in red ink and tab the page.

Because of the project to launder and steal government documents, known in the GO as Operation Snow White, Scientology was involved in a complex court case with the government. The operation name came about because Hubbard considered that once we had finished cleaning the files of those agencies, they'd be snow white, not because of any allusion to the fairy tale.

Scientology assigned private detectives to investigate the backgrounds of the Justice Department attorneys. My job was to take all the information the detectives assembled and summarize it in a series of reports to be used by Scientology attorneys during litigation. It occurred to me that the reports could also be used for blackmail.

One day, as I worked on the floor assembling the timeline of events for the life of a particular Justice Department attorney named Raymond Banoun, I was called into the next room for a meeting.

Dick, my project leader in the GO, led the meeting. "We have a problem," he said seriously, looking at the dozen people assembled in the room. "Meisner's threatening to leak this whole project to the FBI. Not only this one but other GO projects he knows about.

"We can't afford a serious leak of this nature when we're already having major problems with this country's suppressive government. We need a permanent solution to this problem. Does anyone have any suggestions?"

The room was silent.

Finally, someone asked, "Where is Meisner now, Sir?"

"We have him in custody." After a few seconds, he added, "He's being kept in a motel room not far from here. I believe he's been handcuffed to the bed."

"Do you have a plan?" someone asked.

"What would you suggest?" Dick asked.

There was no answer, just an awkward silence.

"Remember," Dick said slowly, his eyes on all of us, "Scientology is the only hope for this planet. If we make it, the planet makes it. If we don't, the planet's doomed. It will be destroyed, reduced to a pile of atomic rubble.

"This one man has the potential, if he does what he says he will, to destroy it all—everything that Hubbard has worked for, and everything that you and I have worked for.

"What can we do? What's the solution? Any ideas?"

"He can't be allowed to escape," a tall woman in the back of the room said. "You can't let him reach the agency and testify. That's all there is to it."

"Yeah, right," someone said. "The greatest good for the greatest number of dynamics. That's what Ron says."

A man on my left said, "What you're saying, Dick, is that it's a no-win situation. Either one person goes, or millions of innocent men, women, and children go. That's the choice, right? Either way, someone has to lose. Isn't that what you're saying?"

We looked at him.

"I'm afraid you're right. That's precisely what we face."

An older man in the back spoke with an English accent. "Take him and dump him overboard at sea with weights. Deep six the bastard."

"Yeah," someone said. "Get rid of him once and for all."

"Any other suggestions?" Dick studied the circle of grim faces.

No one answered.

"Very well. What I can tell you is that the situation will be handled by this time tomorrow. We didn't want any of you to be surprised. If anyone has a problem with this, I expect you to speak up now."

The room was silent.

"All right. There's one other matter. We have a continuing problem with Paulette Cooper. She won't stop her campaign to end Scientology. She's the most deadly Suppressive we have at the moment, a real danger.

"I can tell you that Ron's losing patience with all this. He expects us to handle these things. We simply can't continue to allow one insane person to endanger the survival of everyone else on the planet. She has to be handled. The job of the Guardian's Office is to get Ethics in on the planet so Scientology can expand. Handling these situations is part of the job.

"Any questions?"

I looked around. No one spoke for a long time.

Finally, Dick said, "All right, everyone. Back to work. We're on a tight schedule. Thanks for your time."

I returned to my project. Something about the meeting bothered me, but I pushed those troublesome thoughts from my mind.

"The greatest good for the greatest number of dynamics," I said with a sigh. If it had to be done, it had to be done. I tried to forget it.

Later, I learned that Michael Meisner gained the confidence of his guards and escaped from the motel. He went to the FBI with his information, which resulted in an FBI raid on the Church of Scientology one month later. Eleven Scientologists were indicted and imprisoned, including Hubbard's wife, Mary Sue.

Paulette Cooper was never killed, but the story became very macabre. Apparently, she moved. The story is that a cousin who resembled her took over her old apartment.

One day, a man arrived to deliver flowers. When the cousin opened the door, the man held a gun to her head and cocked it. When it wouldn't fire, he tried to choke her. She managed to scream and flee.

Paulette later reached an out-of-court settlement with the Church.

Years passed. I continued working for the organization in various capacities. I learned calligraphy so I could help inscribe certificates when needed. For a while, I served as the ARC Break Registrar, which meant I had to contact people who were upset with Scientology and offer them free sessions to get them "back on lines." Predictably, I quickly burned out on that job and was transferred to another post, where I was in charge of special events.

The only contact I had with my parents came from occasional letters from them updating me with family news. My brother's marriage and first child, my other brother's graduation from college and teaching position in Europe, my father's heart surgery, my first brother's second and third children, my sister's marriage in Vermont—all were detailed for me. Some of the letters I tossed away without opening, while others I read quickly, refusing to allow myself to feel any emotion.

One day in early 1979, I received a letter from my father telling me that his mother just died. *It's just as well,* I thought callously.

In a session on the PTS/SP Rundown, I identified my grandmother as the main Suppressive on my dad's side of the family. Since she was thoroughly evil, I reasoned, it wasn't necessary to waste any grief on her death.

I received a second letter from my father containing an airline ticket. Would I consider, he wondered, returning to Michigan for my grandmother's funeral? Everyone else in the family would be there.

Something about the idea of a family reunion struck a chord in me. Memories of happy days with my aunts and uncles at the summer cottage, shared by our large, extended family, must've stirred nearly extinct subconscious feelings. I did a very strange thing.

I arranged to take a long weekend from my post, using the excuse of my grandmother's funeral. It was permissible to get leave from post for pressing family matters and was justified as a means of keeping families from becoming openly antagonistic to Scientology.

I made a reservation on a direct flight to Michigan and arrived at the airport well ahead of boarding time. I was one of the first people aboard, and I sat in the last row. Sitting there, as other passengers boarded the plane, I was suddenly seized by an overwhelming feeling of panic and terror.

The flight attendants were just closing the door when I shouted, "Wait! Don't close the door!" I fought my way past other passengers, who were still in the aisles, as people watched in stunned silence.

"I have to get off," I told the attendant nearest the door. "I'm going to be sick. Please," I begged. "Let me off the plane."

She looked forward to the captain, who nodded. She opened the door. I walked down the boarding ramp, and relief flooded over me.

The wog world had become, for me, a place of danger, filled with sinister enemies and suppressives. The hundreds of hours spent listening to Hubbard's ravings on tape had done their job. I was a captive of Scientology. Never again would I voluntarily venture out into the evil wog world.

I mailed the ticket back to my father with an apology.

> I can't come right now. I can't take time off from my post. Tell everyone I said hello.

A month or so later, I received another letter from my father. Perhaps out of guilt, I opened it instead of throwing it away, as I'd done to many other letters from home.

Inside was a certified check made out to me for $20,000. *Enclosed is your inheritance from your grandmother,* I read in my father's scrawling script.

Stunned, I stared at the check in disbelief. Then a wonderful idea came to me—the OT levels. That money would ensure my passage into the realm of OT! I did a joyful dance in front of my coworkers.

Later, I learned that my parents reasoned that, perhaps, with the money to make a fresh start, I might return home. They greatly underestimated, as many parents do, the power of mind control and hypnosis ritualistically enforced over the years through continual repetition of TRs, drills, auditing, propaganda, and the dynamics of group reinforcement in Scientology.

I quickly wrote up a CSW, Completed Staff Work, a petition to my seniors asking for a leave of absence from my post to do the OT levels. I was sure the petition would be approved, especially when it became known I'd just received a substantial inheritance.

I was right. Within the week, I sat in a chair at the desk of the Registrar at the AO, the Advanced Org.

I'd always been awed by the hushed air of excitement at the AO and recalled the many times I'd come into the building to deliver messages or courier packages, dreaming of the day when I'd be there myself to take the upper levels. Now, it was really going to happen.

On the way to the Registrar's Office, I glanced at the pre-OTs sitting quietly in the lobby, waiting for the C/S for their next session.

What do they know? I wondered. *Do some of them actually know the secret of OT 3?* It was well known in Scientology that on the third upper level, Hubbard revealed the great secret of "this sector of the universe," which would explain all human behavior in the world.

The thought that I, too, would soon learn that secret was almost impossible to comprehend. Once I was through the *wall of fire,* the name Hubbard gave to that dangerous and esoteric level, I'd become a "thetan exterior," free from any type of overwhelm for the indefinite and infinite future, able to travel at will outside my body. From there, the possibilities were endless.

"So, you're ready to do the OT levels, yes?" the Registrar, who had a Spanish accent, asked, pulling a folder from his desk drawer.

"Yes." I was almost too excited to talk.

"Very good. Very good, indeed." He smiled and looked through my folder. "The last level you've done is your Grade 4, correct?"

I'd made regular payments through the years into my AP, Advanced Payment, account at the AO and was surprised to see that my credit stood at over $2,000.

"So, first you need to do your Power." He wrote on a pad of paper on his desk. "Because you're on staff, that's half price, or $600." He wrote that number down.

As I watched, a column of numbers took form on his pad.

"And your Solo, which will train you to become a Solo auditor in preparation for the OT levels. Also $600. Of course, you also want to go Clear, right?" He looked at me expectantly.

I nodded. "Of course."

"OK. Clear. $800."

I thought of the speeches I heard at Clear Night. Soon, I'd be making a speech of my own. I shivered at the thought.

"That exhausts your AP account. How much have you received from your grandmother's estate?" He looked at me.

I took the check from my shirt pocket, carefully straightened it, and placed it on the desk facing him.

"So. $20,000. That should get you right on up the chart, I'd think." He didn't seem very impressed, so I assumed he saw checks like that every day. His lack of enthusiasm disappointed me.

"All right," he continued. "Let's do some figuring." He took out a calculator and starting adding and subtracting figures.

"OT 1. That's a short level. You'll probably do that in a day. That's $320." He punched the buttons on the calculator.

"OT 2. $500. And OT 3, right?" He looked at me for confirmation.

"Right." I was determined to match his stoic approach and tried to act as if I spent $20,000 every day.

"OK. $3,000. That's a big level, as you know." He grinned conspiratorially at me.

I grinned back, feeling as if I'd pulled the fabled sword from the stone.

"As for the rest," he continued writing on his pad, "you'll need to have something on account in case you need a review. The balance you'll probably want to leave on account for your remaining levels. Assuming, of course, you plan to continue on up the Bridge." He picked up the check and examined it closely.

"I guess," I said uncertainly. "How much will I have left?"

"After OT 3, that should leave you around $16,000. That's enough to do whatever is C/Sed for you after OT 3. That will give the C/S something to work with.

"And you," he said confidingly, "are about to begin the adventure of a lifetime. Are you ready?"

"Yeah, I'm ready. I've been waiting for this for twelve years. When can I start?"

"You can start by first signing this check." He turned it over and handed me a pen. "Then we'll get you scheduled for your Ethics Clearance right away, maybe even today." He reached for the check after I signed it.

"You'll never regret this." He clapped my shoulder. "You just traded this money," he held up the check, "for the secrets of the universe. Not a bad exchange."

"Wait," I said suspiciously. "What's an Ethics Clearance?" He'd just thrown me a curve.

"It's just routine. Everyone going into the OT levels has to be cleared by Ethics to make sure you have no outstanding Ethics cycles."

"But I haven't had any trouble with Ethics for years," I protested.

"It's just a routine check," he said soothingly. "Look, the OT levels are powerful stuff. If someone tried to do them without ethics, he'd get into a lot of trouble. He might even die. Really, it's for your own good."

All right, I thought. *I'll go along with the program. No Ethics Officer will stand between me and OT 3.*

Soon, I sat opposite the AO Ethics Officer and handed him my Power Routing Form.

"Going up the Bridge?" He was pleasant but businesslike.

I nodded.

"Very well done." He turned on his meter. "We're going to do a couple of security checks. It's just routine to make sure everything is clean before you go to your OT levels." He pulled some plain, white legal paper from a drawer and tested his pen.

"I'll ask you a series of questions," he said. "You don't have to answer. The meter will pick up any reaction you might have to an item. If I get a read, I'll ask you for your considerations, OK?"

"Sure."

"First, I'll ask a few null questions to determine your reaction pattern. Ready?"

"Ready." I felt like an astronaut in a space capsule awaiting launch.

"We will now begin. Are you sitting in a chair?" He looked at me.

I didn't answer. He adjusted the meter.

"Are you on the moon?"

"Have you ever drunk water?"

"Am I an elephant?"

"Are you a table?"

"Good." He looked at me. "You're reading just fine. Now we'll begin the process."

I relaxed.

"Have you ever lived or worked under an assumed name?" He watched the meter. "That's clean.

"Are you here for a different purpose than you say? That's clean.

"Have you ever done any shoplifting? That reads." He looked at me. "Do you have any considerations on that?"

"Yeah." I thought back. "When I was in college, I stole some cigarettes a couple of times from a drugstore. There were some other things—pantyhose, maybe twice. I was just being rebellious. Actually, I felt guilty afterward and mailed money to the store."

"OK. That's clean." He adjusted the meter.

"Have you ever been blackmailed?"

"That's clean.

"Have you ever been in prison?"

"That's clean.

"Are you guilty of anything?"

"That's clean.

"Have you ever embezzled money?"

"That's clean.

"Have you ever been court-martialed?

"That's clean.

"Have you ever had anything to do with pornography?

"That's clean.

"Have you ever peddled dope? That reads. What about that? Have you ever peddled dope?" He looked up.

"Not exactly. I had a boyfriend once who sold marijuana, and sometimes people gave me money to give to him. I didn't sell anything, but I was involved. That's all." I waited for him to clear the question.

"That's clean.

"Have you ever raped anyone or been raped?

"That's clean.

"Have you ever practiced homosexuality?

"That's clean.

"Have you ever had intercourse with a member of your family?

"That's clean.

"Have you ever had anything to do with Communism or been a Communist?

"That's clean.

"Have you ever practiced sex with children?

"That's clean.

"Have you ever taken money for giving anyone sexual intercourse?

"That's clean.

"Have you ever killed or crippled animals for pleasure?

"That's clean.

"Have you ever committed a misdemeanor?

"That's clean.

"Have you ever committed a felony?

"That's clean.

"Have you ever done anything your mother would be ashamed to find out? That reads." He looked at me.

"I'm not sure what it is. I've certainly done things she wouldn't be happy about if she knew about them." I hesitated.

"Like what?"

"Like the affair I had in college. She didn't know about that. I used to smoke marijuana before I got into Scientology."

I closed my eyes and thought. "I had a party in our house once when my parents were away. Some relationships I've had in Scientology. She probably wouldn't approve. That's about all." I yawned.

He asked the question again, then said, "That's clean.

"Have you ever practiced sex with animals?"

"That's clean.

"Have you ever murdered anyone?"

"That's clean.

"Have you ever stolen anything from a Scientology organization?

"That's clean.

"Do you know any Communists personally?

"That's clean."

He asked many other questions. After an hour and a half, I looked at the clock.

"Is there much more?" I asked.

"No. We're almost finished with this check. Try to be patient." He continued with his questions.

"Have you ever had any unkind thoughts about Scientologists? That reads. What about it?" He looked up.

"The Ethics officer at the Org, and a couple people on staff. I had some unkind thoughts about them, but doesn't everybody?"

He checked the question again. "I still get a read. What do you think it might be?"

"I had an unkind thought about Diana Hubbard once. I didn't like her piano playing. At Christmas, I thought it was pretty stingy of Hubbard to just send us some cheese. Sometimes, I resented that the execs at the Org made so much more money than I did."

I thought some more. "Once, I refused to eat the food at the Org. I had unkind thoughts about the cook. I had unkind thoughts about another girl on staff who was going with someone I had a crush on. That's about all I can think of."

"I'll check the question again." He repeated the question. "That's clean.

"What unkind thoughts have you had while I was doing this check? That reads. Anything?"

"No. I just don't like this check. I'm not sure why you have to ask all these things just for me to do the OT levels."

"OK. Are you upset about this Security Check? That reads. Are you upset?"

"Not really. It's just that I didn't know about it, and I thought maybe I could start Power today. I was a little upset, but not badly."

He asked the question again. "OK. That's clean. All right. That's the end of this check. We have one more check to do, but we'll do it after lunch, OK?"

"Fine." I stood and stretched. I wasn't hungry, so I decided to take a walk. It was a beautiful fall day with almost no smog, a rarity for LA.

After lunch, we resumed the session.

"Now we're going to do the Whole Track Sec Check," he said. "Do you know what that means?"

"Since whole track is all your past lives, this must be a sec check of my past lives."

"Good. We'll begin. Have you ever enslaved a population?"

I blinked. "What?" I asked incredulously.

"I'll repeat the question," he said without a reaction. "Have you ever enslaved a population?"

I didn't reply.

"That's clean.

"Have you ever ordered, or committed yourself, genocide?

"That's clean.

"Have you ever annihilated a population?

"That's clean.

"Have you ever upset an ecology?"

"That's clean.

"Have you ever practiced terrorism?"

"That's clean.
"Have you ever bred bodies for degrading purposes?
"That's clean.
"Did you come to Earth for evil purposes?
"That's clean.
"Have you ever made a planet or nation radioactive?
"That's clean.
"Have you ever caused a planet to disappear?
"That's clean.
"Have you ever torn out someone's tongue?
"That's clean.
"Have you ever blinded anyone?
"That's clean.
"Have you ever smothered a baby?
"That's clean.
"Have you ever participated in a sexual relationship between a doll body and a human body?
"That's clean.
"Have you ever made love to a dead body?
"That's clean.
"Have you ever tortured another with electrical or electronic devices?
"That's clean.
"Have you ever been a professional executioner? Clean.
"A brutal jailer? Clean.
"A corrupt judge? Clean.
"An ungrateful child? Clean.
"A wicked mother? Clean.
"A bad father? Clean.
"An abortionist? Clean.
"Have you ever abandoned your sick or dead to the enemy?
"That's clean.
"Have you ever failed to rescue your leader?
"That's clean."

After over 300 such questions, we finished the check.

"Clean as a whistle," the Ethics Officer said. "You're ready to start your Power. Good luck." He initialed my Power Routing Form.

I stood. "Well, I feel better."

He looked up.

"I never knew there were so many things I didn't do. It sort of makes me feel good."

I walked out of the office, glad to be finished with the strange questions.

Conditioned as I was to the bizarre and unusual from my first day in Scientology, I dismissed the events of the day as just another step forward on the Yellow Brick Road to Total Freedom.

I felt like clicking my heels. Soon, I'd be in Oz!

CHAPTER THIRTEEN

We Are All Many

I sat in the lobby of the AO to wait for my first session on the level called Power. Three or four other pre-OTs were also silently waiting. For some reason, there was never much conversation in the AO waiting room.

I looked around at the room. The carpets throughout the building were a deep, royal blue, and the walls were stark white. *The Sea Org colors,* I realized. A bronze, life-sized bust of Hubbard was mounted on a pedestal facing the entrance, keeping silent vigil over all who entered below.

The windows were open, and a breeze, unusually fresh and clean for LA, billowed the curtains and playfully scattered pieces of paper from the desk of Tech Services onto the floor. I reached to retrieve several slips of paper just as a Tech Page called my name.

I followed the boy, who was acting as a page, down the long hallway to a closet-sized auditing room halfway around the building.

My auditor's name was Sandy, a short redhead wearing a Sea Org uniform.

"Pick up the cans, please," she said, wasting no time.

After the usual preliminaries, she began the Power process. "Tell me a source."

"A source." I paused, thinking. "The sun. The sun's a source."

"Good. Tell me about it."

"It gives off heat and light. It provides life energy to the Earth."

"OK. Tell me a no source."

"A rock is a no source. It doesn't give off anything."

"All right. Tell me a source."

I knew the answer. "Me. I'm a source. I have the ability to think, to make postulates, and to carry out those postulates."

"Your needle is floating," Sandy confirmed. "End of process."

"That's it? That's all there is to Power?" I was stunned.

Three minutes and $600 after we began, I was on my way to the Examiner to attest to completing my Power.

Soon, I was routed onto the Solo Course, where I'd be trained as a solo auditor. On the lower levels of Scientology, one was always audited by another person, but, on the upper levels, one audited oneself. Instead of holding the cans in both hands, on the Solo level one held two cans soldered together in one hand while using the other hand to operate the meter and write session notes.

The theory section of the Solo Course was mystifying. The course began with an essay by Hubbard entitled, *The Inner Structure of the Mind.*

> We're going to delineate for you the inner structure of the reactive mind. The core of the reactive mind is the R6 (Routine 6) bank. It is surrounded by engrams and secondaries that must be wiped out to get at the core itself.
>
> What does the R6 bank consist of? You may be surprised to learn it's groups of words called GPMs, Goals-Problems-Mass, which serve to confuse a thetan. They're the cause of aberration. The contents of the R6 bank are aberrant stable data.

According to Hubbard, the reactive mind in each person on Earth was the legacy of millennia of implanting. In the implants, the thetan, between lives, was pinned to a wall with electronic beams and programmed with opposing pairs of words, called *terms* and *oppterms,* while simultaneously being zapped with powerful electronic beams. The result was a permanently crippled and confused thetan who was then returned to Earth to "pick up a new body" and start another lifetime in captivity.

On the Solo Course, one learned to audit those pairs of words and become freed from the devastating effects of the hypothetical implants.

The most interesting skill learned on the Solo Course was the Dating Drill. In that drill, one partner chose a fictitious date, while the other partner, using the E-meter, had to discover the exact date. The date would typically run into the billions or trillions of years.

For example, if my partner chose a date of 260,376,492,790 years, the dating-drill process would go something like this:

"Is the date tens of years, hundreds of years, thousands of years, tens of thousands of years, hundreds of thousands of years, millions of years, tens of millions of years, hundreds of millions of years, billions of years, tens of billions of years, hundreds of billions of years?"

Theoretically, I'd get a small tick on the meter, registering my partner's charge on the correct term, *hundreds of billions of years.* Once that was confirmed, I would narrow it down further.

"Is the date more than 500 billions of years?"
There would be no tick.
"Is the date less than 500 billions of years?"
Tick.
"Is the date more than 300 billions of years?"
No tick.
"Is the date less than 300 billions of years?"
Tick.
"Is the date more than 200 billions of years?"
Tick.

"Is the date more than 250 billions of years?"
Tick.
"Is the date more than 275 billions of years?"
No tick.
"Is the date less than 275 billions of years?"
Tick.
"Is the date more than 260 billions of years?"
No tick.
"Is the date less than 260 billions of years?"
No tick.
"Is the date 260 billions of years?"
Tick.
"Is the date more than 260 billion 500 millions of years?"
No tick.
"Is the date less than 260 billion 500 millions of years?"
Tick.
"Is the date more than 260 billion 300 millions of years?"
Tick.
"Is the date more than 260 billion 400 millions of years?"
No tick.
"Is the date less than 260 billion 400 millions of years?"
Tick.
"Is the date more than 260 billion 350 millions of years?"
Tick.
"Is the date more than 260 billion 375 millions of years?"
Tick.
"Is the date more than 260 billion 380 millions of years?"
No tick.
"Is the date less than 260 billion 380 millions of years?"
Tick.
"Is the date 260 billion 376 millions of years?"
Tick.
"Is the date more than 260 billion 376 million 500 thousand years?"
No tick.

"Is the date less than 260 billion 376 million 500 thousand years?"

Tick.

"Is the date more than 260 billion 376 million 250 thousand years?"

Tick.

"Is the date more than 260 billion 376 million 400 thousand years?"

Tick.

"Is the date more than 260 billion 376 million 450 thousand years?"

Tick.

"Is the date more than 260 billion 376 million 475 thousand years?"

Tick.

"Is the date more than 260 billion 376 million 480 thousand years?"

Tick.

"Is the date more than 260 billion 376 million 490 thousand years?"

Tick.

"Is the date more than 260 billion 376 million 495 thousand years?"

No tick.

"Is the date less than 260 billion 376 million 495 thousand years?"

Tick.

"Is the date 260 billion 376 million 491 thousand years?"
No tick.

"Is the date 260 billion 376 million 492 thousand years?"
Tick.

"Is the date more than 260 billion 376 million 491 thousand years 500 years?"

Tick.

"Is the date more than 260 billion 376 million 491 thousand years 750 years?"

Tick.

"Is the date more than 260 billion 376 million 491 thousand years 800 years?"

Tick.

"Is the date less than 260 billion 376 million 491 thousand years 800 years?"

Tick.

"Is the date more than 260 billion 376 million 491 thousand years 775 years?"

Tick.

"Is the date more than 260 billion 376 million 491 thousand years 780 years?"

Tick.

"Is the date more than 260 billion 376 million 491 thousand years 790 years?"

No tick.

"Is the date less than 260 billion 376 million 491 thousand years 790 years?"

No tick.

"Is the date 260 billion 376 million 491 thousand years 790 years?"

Tick.

"I would like to indicate that the date is 260 billion 376 million 492 thousand 790 years."

While studying the theory section of the Solo Course, I was told I needed a lockable briefcase and a dog leash for the upper levels. I went to J.C. Penney's with the charge card my father gave me to use for limited purchases and bought an inexpensive briefcase. Then I went to the nearest 7-11 store to buy a dog leash.

When carrying the secret upper-level materials, they had to be locked in the briefcase, which was then attached to one's arm via the leash. That was a security precaution to prevent the theft or loss of the greatly valued, confidential upper-level materials.

To do Solo auditing, I locked myself into a room at the house, set up my meter, and began to run the process.

What am I dramatizing? I asked myself.

I had to locate one-half of the word pair I'd been implanted with. For example, I might use the word *smart*. Then I had to find the antonym, *dumb*.

Then I'd read the pair of words aloud until there was no reaction from the E-meter.

"Lazy. Industrious.

"Fat. Thin.

"Quiet. Loud.

"Careful. Careless.

"Isolating. Gregarious.

"Neat. Sloppy.

"Friendly. Unfriendly."

When there were no more words to find, I was finished with Solo. Theoretically, I had a picture of the exact implant structure of my mind.

The Clearing Course was bizarre, containing lists of objects I had to *spot* in my *space*. Some of the objects included hollow triangles going away and coming in, hollow circles going away and coming in, hollow squares going away and coming in, hollow ellipses going away and coming in, hollow cubes going away and coming in, hollow prisms going away and coming in, and hollow cylinders going away and coming in.

That continued through many other shapes.

There were several other bizarre practices.

It might be difficult to understand why approximately 40,000 people in the country and 60,000 overseas would willingly subject themselves to such insane procedures. The only explanation I can offer is that it's quite possible to hypnotize someone to believe anything or perform any action, no matter how ridiculous, without question. The cognitive function of the person's mind is completely disengaged. Can a person's mind be controlled? The answer is yes.

After finishing the Clearing Course, I gave my Clear speech, something to the effect that, "I am happy to finally be At Cause in my life without the burden of the reactive mind that I've been carrying around for thousands of years."

OT 1 consisted of one command—spot a person. I went to a local mall and spotted people for several hours until I came to a *cognition* and realized that I was different from anyone else in the world. At that point, I was finished with OT 1.

OT 2 was another bizarre level on which I had to audit some curious things, including The Arrow, The Woman, The White Black Sphere, Hot Cold, Laughter-Calm, Dance Mob, and the Double Rod. I soon finished and attested to being an OT 2 Completion. I gave my speech to cheers in the AO lobby.

I was ready for the great leap into the Unknown—OT 3, in which I would learn the secret of the universe that had eluded Man for millions of years.

I had a friend, an older man named Les, who volunteered to come with me during my first day on OT 3 and coach me on the materials. We drove to the AO together.

"Nervous?" he asked, lighting a cigarette.

"Yeah, a little. I've only been waiting twelve years to do this level."

"Well, just think, in another hour or so, you'll know the great secret. You'll be one of us." He winked.

At the AO, I first had to find the locked room where the materials for OT 3 were kept, a small closet just across from the OT 3 course room.

I knocked on the door. A slim Sea Org member unlocked the door to let me in, then quickly locked it behind me. I had to unlock my briefcase and show it was empty. He handed me a brown envelope containing the OT 3 materials. I locked it in my briefcase, which was leashed to my arm, and he made sure the latches on the briefcase were secure. Then he let me out of the room and locked the door behind us.

He escorted me across the hall, and I knocked on the door of the OT 3 classroom. The door was unlocked to let me in, then locked behind me. I felt not even the Pentagon had better security than Scientology.

Les had saved me a seat in the classroom. I sat down, unlocked my briefcase, and pulled out the treasured envelope. Smiling at Les, I opened the envelope and pulled out several pages that were photocopies of pages handwritten by Hubbard and began reading.

> The head of the Galactic Federation (76 planets around larger stars visible from here, founded 95,000,000 years ago, very space opera) solved overpopulation (250 billion or so per planet—178 billion on average) by mass implanting. He caused people to be brought to Teegeeack (Earth) and put an H-bomb on the principal volcanoes (Incident II) and then the Pacific-area ones were taken in boxes to Hawaii and the Atlantic ones to Las Palmas and there "packaged."
>
> His name was Xenu. He used renegades. Various misleading data by means of circuits, etc., was placed in the implants.
>
> When through with his crime, loyal officers (to the people) captured him after six years of battle and put him in an electronic mountain trap where he still is. They're gone. The place (Confederation) has since been a desert. The length and brutality of it all was such that this Confederation never recovered. The implant is calculated to kill (by pneumonia, etc.) anyone who attempts to solve it. This liability has been dispensed with by my

tech development.

One can freewheel through the implant and die unless it is approached as precisely outlined. The freewheel (auto-running on and on) lasts too long, denies sleep, etc., and one dies. So be careful to do only Incidents I and II as given and not plow around and fail to complete one thetan at a time.

In December, 1967, I knew someone had to take the plunge. I did and emerged very knocked out but alive, probably the only one ever to do so in 75,000,000 years. I have all the data now, but only that given here is needful.

One's body is a mass of individual thetans stuck to oneself or to the body.

One has to clean them off by running Incident II and Incident I. It's a long job, requiring care, patience, and good auditing. You're running beings. They respond like any preclear—some large, some small.

Thetans believed they were one. This is the primary error. Good luck.

The remaining pages in the packet I'd been given elaborated the detailed procedures to be used in auditing out one's body thetans.

Break came, and I felt very perplexed, as I followed Les from the building.

"Well? What do you think?" he asked eagerly.

I felt very strange. I'd been programmed under hypnosis for twelve years to accept as gospel everything Hubbard said or wrote. I'd paid thousands of dollars to gain access to the privileged OT 3 material. I was programmed to believe, but the materials were too absurd to be believed.

The result was that my mind, like a computer that has come upon data impossible to analyze, refused to compute. I felt as if my mind had been completely shut down. I had the eerie sensation of mental "floating," of being mentally suspended in time and space.

Hubbard had jammed my mind. From that point, I became a total pawn. Unable to think, I was a completely programmable stimulus-response machine, a robot. To use the phrase now popular among ex-Scientologists, I was a "Rondroid."

"I feel sort of strange," I told Les. "I feel like I'm floating. I'm not sure I understand what I just read."

"What didn't you understand?"

"Is he saying that because that guy Xenu millions of years ago blew up thousands of thetans and caused them to become clustered together, that now everyone on Earth is some kind of multiple personality? That what we have to do now is audit all the other thetans stuck to us so they can leave and get their own bodies?"

"Exactly." Les looked at me proudly. "You understand it just fine. You see, everything in Scientology has been leading to this level. The purpose of your lower grades was to erase some of the lighter charge from your mind. Power enabled the dominant being in the 'cluster' to separate so that it—you—could audit the rest of the guys."

"You mean that everyone on the upper levels is just auditing to get rid of their body thetans?" I still felt incredulous.

"Well, you have to appreciate what it'll do for you. You won't believe how good and clean you'll feel after a few hours of OT 3." He put his arm around my shoulder.

"It kind of reminds me of a dog getting rid of its fleas. Somehow, it's not what I expected."

During the remaining days on the course, I learned how to locate and run my body thetans. I had to close my eyes and locate a feeling of pressure somewhere on my body, then telepathically audit the body thetan.

I first audited the thetan through Incident II, which was done by asking the thetan to visualize:

> The area of the atomic explosion (Hawaii or Las Palmas).
> The H-bomb dropped on the volcano.
> The explosion.
> Terrific winds.
> The thetan carried over the peak of the volcano.
> An electronic ribbon coming up.
> The thetan sticking to the electronic ribbon.
> The ribbon pulled down and the thetan implanted.
> A picture of a pilot saying that he is "mocking it up."
> Implant pictures, including God, devil, etc.
> The thetan "cognites" and leaves.

If the thetan didn't leave, if I didn't get a floating needle, then I had to run the body thetan on Incident I, which was described as:

> Loud snap.
> Waves of light.
> Chariot comes out, turning right and left.
> Cherub comes out.
> Blows horn, comes close.
> Shattering series of snaps.
> Cherub fades back (retreats).
> Blackness dumped on thetan.

This implant, according to Hubbard, happened four quadrillion years ago.

I dutifully completed the theory section of the course, then took my E-meter back to the house and began to audit OT 3.

I held the Solo cans in my right hand, leaving my left hand free to work the meter and write my session notes, and closed my eyes.

Soon, I felt a pressure on my head, or imagined I did. There was a flicker on the meter. I concentrated on making telepathic contact with the disembodied being.

"Was it Hawaii or Las Palmas?" I asked the invisible thetan, watching the meter for a reaction.

"Las Palmas. Good."

I had him visualize Incident II. If I saw a floating needle, it meant that the body thetan left me. If the needle didn't float, I had to audit the thetan on Incident I. I tried to do my best with the procedure, but I was soon in trouble.

"You need a review," the Tech Sec (Technical Secretary) said, looking at me seriously.

I walked from the AO back to my house. I was scheduled for a review the following day. I still felt the strange floating feeling. My mind was suspended, and I couldn't think.

Lately, I'd begun to have strange nightmares. I felt increasingly peculiar, and the feelings were getting worse.

In my review, it was found I had overrun the last body thetan I was auditing. That was corrected, and I was sent back to my house to continue the auditing. After several more sessions, I managed to obtain a dial-wide floating needle and was declared an OT 3 Completion.

Where were my gains? Why wasn't I able to leave my body at will, as had been advertised? Where were my psychic abilities?

I began to have an alarming array of physical problems. There was an outbreak of hepatitis at the house. A Health Department nurse came to inoculate everyone living in the house, but I already had a high fever. I was audited to spot the Suppressive to whom I was connected, but nothing came up.

I continued having nightmares. On two occasions, I awoke in the dark, screaming, thoroughly alarming the other people sleeping in the room.

I started having migraine headaches severe enough to keep me in bed the entire day. Even though I took the antibiotics mandated by the Health Department, my fever persisted.

Finally, feeling more dead than alive, I was called into Tech Services.

"I'm afraid you need some more advanced auditing than OT 3," the Tech Sec said. "Some people resolve most of their case on OT 3, but others require an additional auditing procedure."

The auditing I needed was a new level just developed by Hubbard called New Era Dianetics for OTs, or NED for OTs. It cost $8,000 per twenty-five-hour intensive session. Unfortunately, I wouldn't be accepted by the AO for that auditing unless I bought at least two intensives of NED for OTs. In addition, I had to fly to the more advanced AO in Clearwater, Florida, to do the new level.

I was routed back to the Registrar. At that point, I didn't care about the cost. I signed over the balance of my account, $16,000, to the AO. It was all or nothing. I flew to Florida.

In November, 1979, I arrived at Flag, the new Flag Land Base established when Hubbard brought the floating Sea Org ashore several years earlier. I was given a room with two other OTs in the Scientology hotel.

In my first NED session, I learned there were additional body thetans stuck to me that needed to be audited. These BTs hadn't responded to OT 3, because they were unconscious or asleep. Before they could be audited, they had to be awakened.

The sessions continued in the bizarre fashion of OT 3 sessions. First, I closed my eyes and located a "ridge" of sleeping BTs, then I had to flow energy at them until they woke up. Then they could be audited on OT 3.

Finally, twelve years too late, I balked. "No way. This is ridiculous. I can't do this. This isn't what I expected."

From the day I started NED for OTs, my life became a constant Review session. I became increasingly desperate. I panicked as the money and the time in my intensive dwindled without showing any results.

"This isn't working," I complained to the Examiner. "You have to find out what's wrong."

I started complaining to other students working on the same level. "It's not working for me. Is it working for you?"

"Yes," they answered. "It's incredible. I'm having incredible wins."

In the warped logic of Scientology, it was forbidden to think there might be something wrong with the tech. It was forbidden to think or say that the emperor had no clothes.

Therefore, something had to be wrong with me, but what?

One night, I had an especially bad nightmare, and my screams awoke half the building. I was sent for another review.

The following day, I awoke to find a Sea Org member stationed outside my room.

"What's going on?" I asked.

"I've been posted here," she replied. "You've been ordered to stay in your room. Your meals will be brought here."

"But why?"

"Until your case has been straightened out," she answered tersely.

I returned to the room and sat on the bed. *Maybe they're sending me over the rainbow.* Those were Scientology code words to refer to the location, known to only a few select Sea Org members, where Hubbard was in hiding.

At four o'clock that afternoon, my female guard was replaced by another Sea Org member, a stocky male.

Three weeks passed. I paced the room and slept to pass the time.

One night, I looked outside my door and found, to my surprise, my guard, a young uniformed man, was sound asleep. It was after midnight, and the building was quiet.

I crept past him and went out the building's side door, walking nonchalantly past the night watchman.

A block away, I realized I was free, but where could I go? I couldn't go to the Suppressive police. I had no money, and it was almost one o'clock in the morning.

I couldn't think. I walked a few blocks to a small deck on the bay belonging to a nearby condominium complex. Removing my shoes, I sat on the deck and dangled my feet in the cool water.

I looked at the bay with its twinkling night lights. Water lapped rhythmically against the shore. The cloudless sky was filled with stars. It was a picture of complete peace, a soothing contrast to the chaos churning inside me.

I sat there for several hours, trying to think without being able to produce any new options. Eventually, I felt chilled. Slowly, feeling defeated, I walked back to the hotel.

I returned to my room, slipped past the still-sleeping guard, and lay on my bed.

My prison had no locked doors, because they weren't needed. I was imprisoned by the locked doors within my own mind.

One night shortly after my midnight adventure, I was ordered to pack my things. The following morning, I was shuffled into a waiting van. Three guards rode with me in the back of the van.

"Where are we going?" I asked.

"To the airport."

We disembarked at Tampa International Airport, and my guards escorted me to the waiting area for Northwest Airlines. I saw the destination on the board behind the ticket counter—Detroit, Michigan.

"What?" I looked at my guards in confusion.

"We located your parents," one replied in an emotionless voice. "You're returning to Michigan. Here are your instructions." He handed me a thick packet of materials.

The plane was boarding. One of the guards put his hand around my arm and directed me toward the waiting plane. The other two guards disappeared.

I flew to Michigan with my guard, where I found my father waiting at the airport. The guard immediately booked a return flight to Florida.

I rode silently beside my father on the forty-minute drive to Lansing, where my family lived.

I opened the packet I'd been given and found a thirty-page list of instructions.

I was supposed to repay Scientology $30,000 for all services I'd taken as a staff member. I had to read a long list of books and write reviews of each. I was to run, take vitamins, and write a new list of my overts, both in this lifetime and in past lives.

Then I had to retrain on all levels of Scientology. I had to start over as a preclear from Dianetics upward. Once I trained to Class 4 and demonstrated I could again become a valuable member of the group, my petition to rejoin the group would be considered.

I stared at the document in disbelief. Suddenly, the truth exploded in my mind.

I'd been exiled from Scientology.

I'd been offloaded.

CHAPTER FOURTEEN

Back in the Wog World

I sat in the living room of my parents' comfortable house in Michigan, working on a jigsaw puzzle of the Neuschwanstein Castle in Bavaria. The remains of a burning log spat in the fireplace. Outside the large picture window behind me, snow fell softly in the fairyland white world of a Michigan winter.

The first few days back in the wog world were the hardest. The shock of my sudden excommunication from the only world I'd known for twelve years, as well as the already tenuous condition of my mind after months of bizarre upper-level practices of Scientology, combined to create a certain alienation from reality.

The English language, devoid of the liberally sprinkled Scientology words and phrases I was accustomed to, sounded strange to my ears. I had the peculiar feeling, watching TV, that I was somehow listening to a foreign language, though I knew all the words.

I didn't know how to deal with the fact that I was back in the wog world after an absence of twelve years. One night, I gathered all my Scientology certificates I brought with me on the plane and lay them out on my bed. Realizing they had nothing to do with the vocational currency of the wog world, I impulsively took them to the fireplace and burned them one by one, watching, as the fire curled the edges of the heavy papers and transformed them into equally worthless ash.

I was still experiencing the uncomfortable mental phenomena that originated on OT 3. Sometimes, it seemed as if my mind were disintegrating into a thousand tiny pieces that imploded into an internal cosmos. Instinctively, my father bought me the jigsaw puzzle. For two weeks, I did nothing but assemble the intricate pieces. Symbolically, I was attempting to reassemble the scattered fragments of my mind.

I wrote a letter to the Director of Technical Services at Flag and asked if they would please reconsider their action and allow me to return to Flag. One week later, I received a short, terse note. I was told to continue the program they gave me when I left Florida. When that was finished, I could reapply for membership in Scientology. The letter was written on official Sea Org letterhead.

Lacking any better plan, I decided to begin working on the program. I saw no other alternative than to work, no matter how slowly or painfully, back into the good graces of my group.

A few blocks from my parents' house was a busy restaurant. I applied for a job and began waiting tables. I knew my mind was too disorganized to attempt anything more complex. Office work was, at least temporarily, out of the question. I wasn't even able to concentrate enough to read the morning paper. I couldn't extract the meaning from the printed word, a condition that lasted for several months.

I buried myself in restaurant work, signing up for as many hours as possible. Each week, I sent $100 to Flag to be credited toward my debt of $30,000. At that rate, I calculated it would take six years to pay off my debt.

Even though outwardly I was an outcast, in my heart I was still a dedicated Scientologist. I proudly wore my Scientology jewelry to work, and, when anyone asked about it, I launched into a fervent testimonial about the incalculable benefits of auditing.

At home, I buried myself in my Scientology books, working feverishly at the essays I'd been assigned. I lived only for the day when I'd be exonerated and accepted back into the group.

Months passed. I continued at my job and sent my earnings to Scientology. My parents insisted I see a counselor, an act strictly forbidden by Scientology, to whom any mental-health practitioner was a mortal enemy. To satisfy my parents, I finally agreed to some sessions with a social worker at a nearby clinic.

In the year that I met with that counselor, I never once mentioned Scientology. Why should I defend my group to a suppressive enemy who would probably be constitutionally incapable of appreciating the wisdom of Hubbard and his tech?

Eighteen months after being offloaded from Scientology, a new phenomenon began to emerge. I became increasingly irritable at work and home. I was unable to explain my explosive outbursts. Finally, I was forced to take a leave of absence from work.

I had a compulsion to read about other cults. My mind was attempting to heal. Like the young, green plants in spring poking through melting winter snow, my mind and emotions were stirring to life in some unknown subterranean region within. I wrote a new letter to Florida, begging to be allowed to return.

Several weeks later, I received a reply. *We're proud that you're doing so well. Just continue to do well.*

I became increasingly angry as the day wore on. They hadn't answered my questions. Why couldn't I return?

Anger churned in me all day. That night, an unthinkable thought surfaced. I wanted to call a lawyer and sue Scientology.

I was overwhelmed with terror. To sue Scientology was one of the worst suppressive sins. Even the thought was suppressive. Committing a suppressive act would leave me no hope of redemption for trillions of years. Suing Scientology would call down doom upon my soul.

The strange urge persisted. One night, without thinking, I called information for the number of an attorney in Boston who I knew had litigated against Scientology in the past. I was able to reach him and told him my situation. He agreed to consider my case. I had to send him a complete report. He would probably refer the case to an associate of his in Florida, he explained.

My heart pounded as I hung up. I'd done it. It couldn't be undone.

The phone call to the lawyer precipitated a crisis. I became acutely suicidal. I planned to take an overdose of medication I'd been given at the clinic for anxiety. The dose would certainly be fatal.

I emptied the bottle of pills in my hand. The point of no return was a swallow away.

Suddenly, I threw the pills into the sink, grabbed my father's keys, and ran outside to his car. I drove through the city for hours, trying to think. My situation was hopeless—or so it seemed to me.

I stopped at a phone booth and looked through the Yellow Pages. I called the city hospital. "Could someone help me, please?" I begged.

It was a Catholic hospital, and I soon was talking to a priest, Father Steve. He gave me directions to the hospital.

When I arrived, he met me and took me to the cafeteria. Over hot chocolate and out of desperation, I explained my situation. He spent several hours with me, then drove with me to a small house near the university with a sign on the door that read, *Interdenominational Student Center.*

Inside, I met Frank Fuller, the director of the center. It just happened that Frank had recently been researching Scientology. He showed me to a small room in the center with a cot. Exhausted, I slept for over twelve hours.

The following day, Frank sat down with me at the kitchen table and handed me a steaming cup of strong coffee. That cleared my mind. He had with him a stack of papers that he placed conspicuously in front of me.

"We're going to go through some information about Scientology," he explained. "I don't require you to believe everything I show you. I just want to know if you'd be willing to look at some things with me."

Why not? I wondered. I was at a dead end. Moving in any direction had to be better than staying where I was.

"Let's talk about Hubbard," Frank began.

For the next hour, he told me things about Hubbard I never knew. He wasn't the person he portrayed himself to be.

Point by point, we went through Hubbard's biography that I'd learned while in the cult. According to Frank, almost everything

Hubbard said about himself was a lie, and Frank had the documents to prove it.

His grandfather, I read, didn't own a cattle ranch one-fourth the size of Montana. Hubbard grew up in a house in an average small Montana town. He didn't travel extensively in Asia as a teenager. His travels were mostly in his imagination. He wasn't the decorated war hero he portrayed himself to be. In fact, his war record was deplorable. At the end of the war, he was in a Navy psychiatric ward.

There were hundreds of such lies.

"But why would he lie to us?" I asked incredulously. *It's true,* I realized. *I never questioned the things he said about himself.* Such an idea had never occurred to me. I had just blindly believed.

I looked at the failing transcript of Hubbard's college record. He told us he was one of the first students of nuclear physics. According to his transcript, he failed the course. There was a damaging letter he wrote to the Veteran's Administration, begging for psychiatric help, complaining of *periods of moroseness and suicidal inclinations.*

I sat with Frank for hours that day, as my god was systematically dethroned. Hubbard, I learned, was a bigamist and a Satanist. He'd been married simultaneously to his first and second wives. Frank showed me proof that Hubbard was deeply involved in the occult, performing satanic rituals devised by his mentor, the English Satanist Aleister Crowley.

I still couldn't let go.

Hubbard was a habitual drug user, under the influence of which most of the Scientology catechism had been written. In that light, I thought, books like *The History of Man* made more sense. He had a habit of using affirmations that he repeated every day. One of those was, "All men shall be my slaves! All women shall succumb to my charms! All mankind shall grovel at my feet and not know why!"

After a few days, I returned home feeling confused, stunned, and betrayed. Why had I never questioned any of those things? Why had I accepted everything without thinking?

Much later, I arrived at the answer to those questions. At the age of seventeen, I was naïve and gullible. I'd been raised in a system in which I was programmed to accept the words of adults without question. My parents and teachers had always been right. I made the fatal unconscious assumption that, since I was honest and had good motives, others must be, too. As a teenager, I'd never been disillusioned or deceived. I was unprepared for a monster like Hubbard, who knowingly used hypnosis and mind control to entrap me to exploit me for his own purposes.

The turning point came one day in October, 1981. Frank took me to a deserted church where we sat in the empty pews, and I soaked in the long-forgotten comfort of the religion I abandoned many years before encountering Scientology. I knew in my mind I had to choose who would be my god. Would it be Hubbard, or would it be the God of my childhood Whom I had abandoned?

I knew the answer. Hubbard was no longer worthy of godhood. Strangely and miraculously, having made my choice, I suddenly snapped out of the hypnotic trance I'd been in for twelve years. I literally woke up, as if an invisible hypnotist snapped his fingers. From that moment, I knew I'd never return to Scientology.

A decision began to emerge. I'd return to Florida to talk to the attorney to whom I'd been referred by the Boston lawyer. Over the ensuing weeks, my resolve hardened into action.

In November of that year, I returned to Clearwater. The attorney accepted my case. Ten years later, my case against the Church of Scientology was still pending.

Coming to know the truth about Scientology was not the end of my problems. It took me ten years and hundreds of hours of counseling to come to terms with my experience in Scientology and to deal with the anger I felt toward the man and the organization responsible for my exploitation and betrayal.

I still have nightmares about Scientology. The healing process continues.

I'm free. Having once been deceived by a master of deception, I can never be deceived the same way again. I'll never again sign away the deed to my mind to anyone, no matter how convincing he might be.

My freedom was purchased at a tremendous cost. Neither my freedom nor my mind will ever be for sale again.

EPILOGUE

Blood on the Bedroom Wall

Fighting against Scientology can be hazardous. Since initiating litigation against them ten years ago, I've learned new meanings for the word *harassment,* ranging from the macabre to the ridiculous.

One steamy Florida summer's night several years ago, I returned to my apartment late and found the door wide open. No one was inside, and nothing seemed disturbed. However, when I entered the bedroom, I saw a dark-red liquid had been splashed against the wall just beside the bed. It was blood, still wet and dripping.

Scientologists have come to my apartment or accosted me at the mall where I worked. Sometimes, they called my boss and asked from which door I would be leaving. Occasionally, they waited for me and came up to me as I walked to my car.

Twice they threatened my life. "If you don't drop your lawsuit against the Church," I was told, "you know what'll happen to you."

They didn't use the word *kill.* They didn't have to. From my experience working for the Guardian's Office, now renamed the Office of Special Affairs, I knew what they meant.

Twice my car has been vandalized. I've received threatening phone calls at all hours of the day and night. Ominously, mail has been sent to my siblings who have small children. In the most recent campaign against me, someone has been leaving my phone number on the pagers of various men in the city, resulting in some curious late-night calls.

My old friend Antonio is still alive, and, to my knowledge, still in Scientology. Aileen, the lovely lady who was the founder of Celebrity Center in Los Angeles, died fifteen years ago from a brain tumor. She remained until her death a dedicated and loyal Scientologist.

I believe Scientology to be one of the most, if not *the* most, vicious of the three thousand or so cults in the United States today. I believe that many Scientologists, if they knew their mission on Earth was doomed to failure, would willingly commit suicide on command. There are rumors that one of the secret upper levels contains suicide training. If that's true, Jonestown would pale in comparison with the potential for disaster in Scientology.

Most Scientologists are good, loyal, and well-meaning, though misguided, people. Most of them are very likeable. All Scientologists are fanatics about one thing—Scientology. As many parents have discovered, they are impervious to reason about that one subject due to their years of hypnotic training.

Parents are helpless against Scientology. Deprogramming, the one effective way of extracting a loved one from that cult, is illegal, because restraining someone against his or her will is considered kidnapping, a felony under United States law. The fact that a loved one, often a minor, has been psychologically kidnapped by a cult, and, in the case of Scientology, hypnotized without knowledge or consent, isn't taken into consideration in the courts. Hopefully, over time, that will change.

My life is different in many subtle ways because of my experience in Scientology. I have psychological scars similar, I believe, to someone who's been raped. I have frequent nightmares about the cult. I feel deceived and betrayed on many different levels—mentally, emotionally, spiritually, and financially. I'll never again trust in the same way I did before Scientology.

There are other scars. It isn't possible for me to see displays of Hubbard's books in bookstores, especially *Dianetics,* which has successfully lured thousands of unsuspecting people into Scientology, without feeling a sense of revulsion. I have the same reaction to the Scientology ads on TV. I feel a certain anger and the sense of powerlessness of a victim.

Last week, I was wandering through the flea market of a local university. Once a week, the university sponsors an open-air flea market where vendors can sell their wares, and students can buy inexpensive clothes, plants, and books. I noticed a new display from a young man selling Dianetics books to students.

I watched as a young woman of seventeen or eighteen listened raptly to the Scientologist's spiel. There was a forlorn air about her, the air of someone lost and seeking. Instantly, I felt thrust into a time warp, as I watched myself twenty-some years earlier listening transfixed to a beguiling message of hope and promise.

I—she—reached for the book and walked away.

"Excuse me!" I ran after her through the crowded market.

She looked at me in surprise.

"That book you have." I pointed at the Dianetics book. "It's about a dangerous cult called Scientology. I know, because I was in it for twelve years."

She looked suspicious.

"Look," I pleaded, desperate to save her and myself. "Here. I'll give you the five dollars you paid for the book. You don't need it. It's a cult. I don't want you to go through what I've been through."

She smiled and handed me the book. "Fine." She accepted my money. "Thanks." She disappeared into the crowd.

I walked to the trash bin and buried the book deep inside. Then I, too, turned and walked into the crowd.

If only someone had been able to warn me, I thought.

I had the great satisfaction of knowing that, because of my experience, there would be one less victim of Scientology.

That one is enough.

Margery Wakefield lives in Denver, Colorado, where she works as a caregiver.

    She can be reached at:
    PO Box 100932
    Denver, Colorado 80250

2073754R00123

Printed in Great Britain
by Amazon.co.uk, Ltd.,
Marston Gate.